Identity Work
in the Classroom

Identity Work in the Classroom

Successful Learning in Urban Schools

Cheryl Jones-Walker

Foreword by Theresa Perry

TEACHERS COLLEGE PRESS

TEACHERS COLLEGE | COLUMBIA UNIVERSITY

Published by Teachers College Press, 1234 Amsterdam Avenue, New York, NY 10027

Copyright © 2015 by Teachers College, Columbia University

Library of Congress Cataloging-in-Publication Data

Jones-Walker, Cheryl.
  Identity work in the classroom : successful learning in urban schools / Cheryl Jones-Walker ; foreword by Theresa Perry.
    pages cm
    Includes bibliographical references and index.
    ISBN 978-0-8077-5691-1 (pbk.)—ISBN 978-0-8077-5692-8 (case)—ISBN 978-0-8077-7407-6 (ebook)
    1. Education, Urban—United States. 2. Teacher-student relationships—United States. 3. Identity (Psychology) in children—United States. 4. Identity (Psychology) in adolescence—United States.
    LC5131.J66 2015
    370.9173'2—dc23

                                                                           2015022359

ISBN 978-0-8077-5691-1 (paper)
ISBN 978-0-8077-5692-8 (hardcover)
ISBN 978-0-8077-7407-6 (ebook)

Printed on acid-free paper
Manufactured in the United States of America

22 21 20 19 18 17 16 15   8 7 6 5 4 3 2 1

To Khari, Micah, and Xan—each extraordinary in your own way, not unlike the young people whom we are failing to educate in cities across the United States

Cultural identity . . . is a matter of "becoming" as well as of "being." It belongs to the future as much as to the past. It is not something which already exists, transcending place, time, history, and culture. Cultural identities come from somewhere, have histories. But like everything which is historical, they undergo constant transformation.

—Stuart Hall

Contents

Foreword

Identity Work in the Classroom: Successful Learning in Urban Schools is an extraordinary and compelling book. It is essential reading for teacher-educators, teachers, and community organizers. This book is a refreshing departure from education books that talk about urban schools from afar and with little specificity.

Cheryl Jones-Walker takes us into classrooms and allows us to see up-close the work of two outstanding urban teachers, one Black and one White, and in two different disciplines, math and language arts. She gives us access to how they think about their work, organize their classrooms, structure classroom discourse, select curricular choices, engage in conversations with their students, and how their students respond to their teaching. We learn how these two teachers, in distinct and similar ways, coconstruct identities as teachers who are committed to providing access, creating opportunity, and preparing their students to be successful in the world. We also discover how their identities are inflected and informed by their life histories, education, and current work as teachers. The details captured in Jones-Walker's field notes and in the book—the actual words and emotions of teachers and students, the way she cross-references what she hears by talking to students or teachers—is reflective of the substantial amount of time she has spent in the teachers' classrooms and schools. *Identity Work in the Classroom* represents the best of contemporary critical school ethnography.

In this book, we are transfixed by the conversations that the author has with each teacher about how each of them separately, in conversations about or with their students, had unwittingly reproduced hegemonic narratives about their students—for example, "the fearful Black man" and "lazy Black students." We hear how each teacher reacts when Jones-Walker brings these incidents to their attention. In reading the text, we imagine each teacher engaging in the ongoing process of identity construction. The power and beauty of this book lies in the author's willingness to lay bare the accomplishments along with contradictions and anxieties of the teachers—individuals who are in the process of their ongoing development.

It is important to note that the two teachers had the benefit of a study group, as the author invited each teacher to suggest teachers from their respective schools to join a cross-school study group on identity making in the context of their teaching. Deans of schools of education and chairpersons of teacher education departments would benefit enormously from reading this book; it could potentially challenge administrators who work in cities to make teacher study groups an essential part of their university-school partnerships.

Throughout the book, Cheryl Jones-Walker reminds us that the kind of teaching these teachers engage in, the relationships they build with their students, and the innovative curricular and pedagogical decisions they are able to make are not available to most urban teachers. They have been afforded this privilege/autonomy because they teach in successful schools and have accomplished much with their students—as measured by state and federal accountability standards.

The author begins and ends the book by forcing us to pay attention to the larger sociopolitical context in which these two teachers and other teachers in city schools do their work. In a comprehensive review of research, Jones-Walker lays bare the sinister nature of the narrative and policies that have framed urban school reform for over 2 decades. She convincingly argues that instead of moving us toward educational equity, these reforms—from NCLB to Race to the Top to the Common Core Initiative—have created failure by undermining, constraining, and cannibalizing the activity that is the heartbeat of excellent schools—the intellectual work, identities, passions, and expertise of teachers and their students.

This is, however, a hopeful book. Particular aspects of the teachers' practice that are responsive to the lives of the students—the Unit of the Harlem Renaissance, the Neighborhood Study that is based on Dubois' *Philadelphia Negro*, especially and how the units inform the teaching and learning and of students and teachers—will make you immediately want to find someone with whom you can discuss the book. In conclusion, the author examines the work of teachers who are insurgents in the face of the governmental and market forces that aim to constrain teaching and learning in urban schools and redefine the nature of public schools. These teachers and others similarly situated have organized their classrooms as communities of teaching and learning, such that membership itself means being an achiever. They have created classrooms where their students coconstruct identities of achievers—identities that are coincident with their racial, ethnic, and social-class identities.

—*Theresa Perry*

Acknowledgments

While completing this book project is deeply satisfying, I have frequently admitted to friends and colleagues that I may not have taken on the task if I had had a real understanding of the time it would take from proposal to publication. I have learned a lot in this process and I am grateful for the wisdom, encouragement, and examples set by those close to me. I have been lucky to be in an intellectual and collaborative community over the past 8 years at Swarthmore College, and I have grown tremendously as a teacher and researcher because of my interactions with students, departmental colleagues, members of the Black Studies program, and compatriots in practice. Since production of scholarly work can feel like such a solitary practice, I cherish those people who helped me find another model, whether it was cowriting with Anita Chikkatur and Kathy Schultz or coteaching with Frank Grossman and debating with him about the ideas that would find their way into my writing. Working alongside Ellen Clay, Lauren Silver, or Rachel Burma brought unexpected insights because each worked in different fields and would stimulate my thinking, help me make important interdisciplinary connections, and at the same time keep me focused on the end goal while providing wonderful company.

The beauty of bringing this project to a close was the way that my interests, passions, and professional and personal goals collided as I filled the pages of this book. Teaching undergraduates is a generative process, and both the teaching and mentoring processes give me a chance to engage in the kind of work I describe as so important to developing individuals, improving institutions, and changing our social world. One tension I have felt, particularly while raising small children, is whether engaging in discussions, preparing socially conscious scholars and teachers, or producing a manuscript is the right focus in a moment when public educational systems in urban communities is in jeopardy.

I am incredibly appreciative for my family of origin (the Joneses) and the one created when I fell in love with Noland (the Walkers) and gave birth to our three sons. While I am often stunned by the requirement of time and emotional energy that our boys demand, they constantly remind me of my great fortune, and I am glad that not only am I nudged into being my best self but also into leading a more balanced life. My family of friends—

sprinkled as near as Philadelphia, New York City, Washington, DC, and Boston and scattered as far as Oakland, Johannesburg, Grenada, and Honolulu—have contributed to keeping things in perspective and helped me make a meaningful life. Andrea Harris Smith, Simone White, Jacquie Jones, and Imani Perry have taught me so much about identity and representation through law and literature, film and media, poetry and theater.

Valuable research and feedback was provided by a number of my students, including Charmaine Giles, Hana Lehmann, and Shameika Black, in addition to the students of the Changing Schools, Changing Communities seminar (Alis, Cortnie, Steve, Rebecca). I valued the editorial assistance (and countless other gifts) provided by Harlan and Tanya Jones. I also want to extend a heartfelt thank you to Barbara Ray, from Hired Pen, who supported the early development of this manuscript. Finally, the project could not have been completed without the incredible guidance from Emily Spangler at Teachers College Press. Her patience, even temperament, clear communication, and professional expertise was a welcomed support during this process.

CHAPTER 1

Introduction

Policies are, in part, discourses—values, practices, ways of talking and acting—
that shape consciousness and produce social identities.

—P. Lipman (2011, p. 11)

Failure hangs in the air, its potency so great that it has begun to cloud the
vision of even those who claim a sense of clarity when it comes to issues of
teaching and learning. Educational reformers have been at work for more
than 2 centuries, and most recently their focus has turned to urban schools
and systems. Current models favor choice, corporate management, and rigid
accountability regimes (Apple, 2001). Many policymakers and administrators have taken a get-tough approach in the battle to improve students' and
schools' progress, and the index for performance most often applied is standardized assessment. Despite the many different approaches, strategies aimed
at improving schools in urban districts have yielded very few successes for
the majority of students. The consequences are severe; although the threats
of withdrawn funding due to failure to make "adequate yearly progress"
(AYP) have loosened with the arrival of No Child Left Behind (NCLB) waivers, the pressure faced by city schools and districts has continued to grow.

Educators regularly ask why students are failing at such high rates and
why the large achievement gap between students in urban school districts
and their peers in suburban and private schools persists. This line of inquiry often leads to theories about the culture produced by poverty, families'
values regarding education, and students' capacities for learning. But I believe we are asking the wrong questions. Rather than asking why students
are failing, we should look at the *construction* of success and failure in our
schools. Rather than students failing or teachers failing students, it might be
the very reforms designed to improve student achievement that are setting
schools up for failure. Varenne and McDermott (1999) investigate the discourse around schooling in America and argue that categorizing success and
failure "can [n]ever capture the good sense of what children do. They directly conspire to prevent all of us from understanding the conditions within
which the child's life is constructed" (p. 3).

Underlying reforms to date has been an unspoken and paternalistic assumption that neither administrators nor teachers in inner-city schools are knowledgeable or talented enough to successfully run these systems. Neither students nor their parents are viewed as having an important perspective to offer in terms of what changes could be made to support students' needs and improve engagement. Often there is a misconception that urban students are not as capable and their families are not as invested in education as their White and middle-class peers. Whether this logic leads to asserting more and more control over administrators and school staff or to creating the rationale to dismantle the public school system (Lipman, 2011), the effect is the same: the lives and educational needs of students go ignored.

A general distrust of teachers' professional ability and students' intellectual acumen has led to increasingly prescriptive reforms that leave very little space for students and teachers to know one another beyond a superficial level. While there has been an admission that the rigid and top-down nature of reforms of the past decade has depressed instruction rather than elevating it, the implementation of recent policies seem to be trending in the same direction. So, in the place of strict pacing guides, we now have a Common Core that suggests standards and goals rather than content and pedagogy. In either case, the context and pressure of such mandates stifles the development of deep relationships. Proponents of the Common Core State Standards (CCSS) may imagine the possibility for more innovation and increased opportunity for teacher-designed curricula, but the rush to assess teachers' and students' progress with these newly designed curricular materials before they are aligned with new assessments constrains teachers' ability—to design instruction based on students' backgrounds, interests, and needs—in familiar ways. These pressures can be overwhelming for teachers and often impede their ability to engage in critical processes for learning: building relationships, listening, taking an inquiry stance, and making school relevant to students' lives. One preservice teacher expressed her concerns about prioritizing the expectations set forth by her teacher education program and those practices required by the school district. She posed the following question in a focus group comprised of other preservice teachers in her cohort:

> They keep telling you, you should do this, you should do this. How do teachers actually . . . do all that stuff at once? How [do] you actually cover the material you need to, and make it exciting and teach for understanding and be culturally sensitive, and you know, encourage children, validate children's own experiences and all this stuff? I don't understand how anyone gets anything done. There's too much stuff to think about. (Quoted in Schultz, Jones-Walker, & Chikkatur, 2008, p. 156)

The need to negotiate an array of changing mandates that come from district, state, and increasingly federal policy initiatives makes the already challenging work of a teacher seem impossible. If a teacher is led to believe that any departure from new curricular adoptions will jeopardize students' ability to demonstrate proficiency on Common Core tasks and Common Core assessments, then teachers will likely forgo what they understand to be good teaching because it appears incompatible with required mandates and allotment of instructional time. Dedicating class time to learning about students' home lives or adopting alternative classroom structures or curricula that have previously been shown to increase student engagement may seem like too great a risk. Some teachers have the latitude to reteach a lesson, supplement district materials, or substitute an alternative instructional plan, but many do not. Teachers who have autonomy typically demonstrate success in making learning gains, which are reflected in standardized test scores and a variety of other measures. These teachers tend to succeed because they are confident about their teaching decisions and instructional practices, and they often subvert the required mandates (Jones-Walker, 2008).

Logically, we should examine the pedagogy of teachers who have met success and encourage other teachers to adopt these approaches, rather than make exceptions for a few teachers and increase the likelihood that they will close their doors in the interest of protecting students' education. Students are performing well when instructed by teachers who have autonomy, in part because of the talent and commitment of these educators, but also because these teachers can bring their whole selves and their professional judgments to the classroom. As a result of recent changes in educational systems, it has become increasingly difficult for teachers to get to know their students as learners (and as people in the world) and then make instructional decisions based on their own background and knowledge and the academic and social experiences of their students.

It has long since been established that to be an effective teacher, one must individualize instruction (Cuban, 1986; Edmonds, 1979; Gutierrez, 1992); however, current policies leave no room for individualization, despite our nation's rhetorical commitment to leave none of our children behind. Reformers are now focused on developing rigorous curricula that are aligned to the CCSS and building new tasks (or activities) to assess the degree to which students have mastered these standards. No sooner were these standards adopted with the intention of breathing life, variety, and breadth back into the curriculum than they became the new tool of accountability and evaluation of teachers. It is challenging for a teacher to familiarize herself with a new set of standards, align a curriculum to the CCSS, think about the best assessment strategies, and innovate in ways that will speak to the interests of learners. The approach taken in many states raises questions about implementation because the rollout, assessment, and accountability too closely mirror the pitfalls of NCLB. With this pressure, many teachers will be forced into focusing on coverage (so that students are afforded equal access to curricula) rather than designing for the conditions that would afford mastery of content. In truth, some students need more time, some must be retaught, some require a different strategy in order to understand a concept, and still others must see how lessons connect them as a person to the larger world.

This book reminds us that we must take into account the social identities of the learner (e.g., race/ethnicity, class, gender) in order to produce successful outcomes for students. In addition, teachers must reflect upon their own identities and beliefs because pedagogical decisions flow directly from belief systems formed in large part through early life experiences. The case has been made for the inextricable link between identity and learning (Drake, Spillane, & Hufferd-Ackles, 2001; Jones-Walker, 2008; McCarthey & Moje, 2002; Wortham, 2006). Identity construction refers to the ways in which an individual's experiences, social group membership, and position within social contexts together inform how a person thinks about and represents him- or herself. The dialogic nature of identity-making means that not only does how a person self-identifies inform his way of being but the interactions with others and the ways in which he is perceived by others will play a part in his conception and definition of self (Gee, 2004; McCarthy, 2001). Identity development is therefore a phenomenological process (Spencer & Markstrom-Adams, 1990).

This book outlines how schools can be a critical site for the positive construction of identities, as well as a critical first step to improvement in learning and more expansive educational and professional opportunities. My aim is to broaden the ways we think about identity construction and make the variety of sites and multiple levels of identity-work more visible. There are daily choices that teachers, students, parents, and school officials make that are connected to the roles that these individuals occupy and the contexts that they shape. Through these daily decisions—coming to school, resisting a policy, and creating classroom discourse—people are contributing to the identity-making of individuals and institutions.

DEFINING IDENTITY

Although definitions of identity are frequently contested, I borrow Levinson and Holland's (1996) framing, which views it as a dialogic process, one that is constituted in practice through interactions between institutions and people. This framing, which highlights the fluid, context-dependent, temporal, and overlapping nature of identity construction, improves when merged with critical social theories that posit that a consistent sense of self persists when practiced and enacted across contexts (Essed & Goldberg,

2002). In negotiating two discrete frameworks (cultural production and critical social theories of race) that are admittedly in tension, I propose a conceptualization of identity that is at once micro and macro, structural and cultural, material and ideological, ascribed and self-ascribed. Too often, models of identity consider that we must focus on large-scale structures or person-to-person exchanges rather than taking into account how microlevel interactions are informed by larger sociohistorical models and act together to inform individuals and the spaces they inhabit. In the descriptions of classroom interactions and school-level practices in the latter half of this chapter, identity-work encompasses these dualities, which are often set as opposing poles on a continuum.

Throughout the book, I refer to this process as "identity-making" or "identity-work." The features or key aspects of identity-making apply to the work of the teacher and the learner and include the activities that appear in Table 1.1. While it is essential to provide the constitutive elements of identity-work, it is a complex process rather than a set of discrete outcomes; therefore, the sum of its parts does not necessarily add up to the whole.

This book provides a window into how teaching and learning can look when educators are committed to knowing themselves and their students in spite of rigid district, state, or federal policies. Reflecting on their own identities and beliefs can prove to be enlightening to teachers in terms of their pedagogical approaches, as these decisions are informed by early life experiences. Interactions with students can influence teachers, but more significant is the influence on teachers' identities and the practice of engaging in structured conversations with colleagues. In the current context of urban schools, this approach is difficult, and occasionally impossible.

Two teachers, Dr. Ellen Clay and Ms. Andrea Carter provide the central examples in this book. (Names of all teachers and students used in this book are pseudonyms, except for Ellen.) I selected their schools as research sites because one mirrored the district demographics and the other was more diverse, better resourced, more autonomous than other district schools, and served a higher proportion of middle- and upper-middle-class students despite the fact that there were only five city blocks between them. In many ways it was the educators rather than the schools who captured my attention because of their interest in exploring identity and reflecting on their practice. Each teacher was asked to invite other colleagues to participate in a study of teacher and student identities through a cross-school study group. Ellen and Andrea's own credentials and effectiveness—reinforced by the high standardized test scores of their students—provided them far more flexibility and autonomy than most teachers in urban school districts.

Not all teachers have the freedom Andrea and Ellen do, and standardized test scores should not be the only criterion used to determine whether teachers gain the freedom to modify curricula in order to meet students' needs. This yardstick requires exceptional educators; unfortunately, good

Table 1.1. Aspects of Identity Work

Student Identity-Making	Teacher Identity-Making
Discussing one's background and beliefs with teachers and student colleagues	Discussing one's background and beliefs with students and colleagues
Talking about how experiences (background) shape beliefs, attitudes toward schooling, and stance as a learner	Talking about how experiences (background) shape beliefs, teaching philosophy, teaching practice
Participating in conversations about social identities (race, class, gender, nationality, religion) and societal structures	Facilitating conversations about social identities and societal structures
Examining one's positionality within the classroom, school community, home community and larger world	Examining one's positionality within the classroom, school community, and larger world
Making your interests, perspectives and needs known in ways that might inform your learning experiences	Exploring students' interests, beliefs, and experiences in order to shape the curriculum and to make it more dynamic
Drawing connections between academic work and events and activities outside of school	Connecting academic content to events and intellectual work that happen outside of school
Reflecting on interactions, actions, and choices in relation to the experiences and circumstances of others	Reflecting on interactions, actions, and choices in relation to the experiences and circumstances of others

teachers, or those who are developing their instructional practice, are rarely afforded the conditions in which to become excellent and achieve the established goals. Despite the fact that the focal teachers are more credentialed, effective (evidenced by a range of measures) and agentive than the average teacher, they are illustrative of opportunities and challenges represented in classroom-, school-, and district-based identity-work.

Even when qualified and committed teachers are allowed to pursue an alternative approach to meeting mandated curriculum standards, and even when they are able to recognize that their identities and those of their students are of consequence, identity-work can be challenging. The incidents, interactions, and curricular choices that follow are presented in order to describe the type of identity-work that can occur in classrooms when teachers are given instructional freedom but also how complicated and uncomfortable this work can be. When we turn our gaze toward unpacking student–teacher interactions and the construction of identities in the context of learning, exquisite moments move to the background and tricky, tension-filled ones take center stage. The stories in this book reveal the difficult nature of engaging those issues related to social identity that I argue must be attended to if we want to improve student performance. The reality is that in the current educational context, progress requires an exceptional teacher who will willingly open up the classroom as a place to interrogate the roles that race, gender, class, nationality, and religion play in the process of teaching and learning.

Given that identity-work is challenging, it is critical that the policies we create support successful approaches rather than force teachers to work around the system by ignoring or resisting mandates. We must design reforms that support creative instruction because identifying and responding to the needs of students in urban schools has been shown to be the lynchpin of success (Ladson-Billings, 2009). This step is critical if we are to retain good teachers, if we hope to see increases in student learning, and particularly if our goal is to make large-scale improvements that are sustained over time. Who teachers are—their backgrounds, experiences, and beliefs—is central to the project, not alone but in relation to and in interaction with the experiences, backgrounds, and identities of the students they teach.

THE STUDY

Driven by an interest in the experiences of teachers and students in urban schools, I conducted a critical ethnography based on two classrooms in neighboring K–8 schools. I was able to immerse myself in the classrooms, communities, professional development sessions, school assemblies, and, on occasion, fieldtrips. After spending approximately 200 hours as a participant observer, I made connections between teachers' goals and practices and could determine the sense their students made of the interactions and circulating discourses in each context. Life history interviews conducted with six teachers allowed me to trace teachers' identities to their beliefs and demonstrate how these belief systems informed their instructional goals and decisions.

Through observations, artifact collection, student and teacher interviews, and focus groups, I was able to uncover constraints and opportunities resulting from interactions between students and teachers in classrooms in a large urban school district. My goal for this book is to answer the call made by Varenne and McDermott (1999) to expose critical work that makes meaning of individuals' daily lives and that can inform our work

toward larger educational reform. The authors make the following obser-
vation:

> It is only by doing this critical work, systematically and painstakingly, that the
> questions we ask of ourselves can be answered albeit temporarily, and, more im-
> portant, transformed. In the routine performance of their everyday lives, people
> seldom answer directly questions about wide-scale constraints on their lives. . . .
> Rather, they point at those aspects of their environment that are most salient to
> what they must be doing. By struggling, always to look more carefully at what
> people point to, we indeed have a chance to transform our understanding and
> our efforts at reform. (p. 20)

ORGANIZATION OF THE BOOK

Chapter 2 of this book will demonstrate the inextricable link between
identities and learning using examples from two urban classrooms to reflect on the trends observed by other scholars. The chapter links various
elements and definitions of identity construction in ways that complicate
current theoretical frameworks. Mapping teachers' life history interviews
with classroom based-examples, I show identity construction to be a dynamic and dialogic process. Poststructural definitions of identity (fluid,
context-dependent, temporal, multiple/overlapping) become more satis-
factory when merged with critical social theories that point to the fact
that a consistent sense of self persists when practiced and enacted across
contexts.

Chapters 3, 4, and 5 present interventions that can be made at the classroom level, as well as at the school level, through curriculum, participant
structures, and discourse. First, in Chapter 3, I focus on curricular interventions and the required shift from teachers implementing curriculum as a
way to cover core standards to teachers building relationships with students
that lead to the intellectual inquiry that will support them as learners in and
out of the classroom. In Chapter 4, I highlight how classroom discourse
around social equity and inequity are framed by teachers and understood
by students.

Chapter 5 examines the goals articulated by a group of teachers and the
way district-based reforms impede their ability to engage in identity-work.
Expert educators engaged in networks with other reflective practitioners are
able to find ways to bring alternative curricular materials and instructional
strategies to their classrooms, but this requires working around the system,
bending—and occasionally ignoring—elements of required mandates. The
alternative steps they take are related to students' identities, how teachers
view school, the relationships they develop with individuals, and what plans

students articulate for their futures. These teacher networks are in some instances school-based, in others citywide, and occasionally connected to national teacher projects; they provide the space for reflection, collaboration, and supports that are necessary for instructional improvements.

Chapter 6 is framed around the insights of teachers and students in order to reimagine the role of teachers, curricula, and schooling more generally as they simultaneously direct our efforts when restructuring policies for the most optimal learning outcomes and life experiences of all learners. In this chapter I urge the reader to consider why these voices are marginalized and what is at stake in processes of educational reform. It is here that I consider the identities of public educational institutions more generally and what it will take to reimagine the possibilities for urban schools.

The concluding chapter, Chapter 7, outlines the implications of identity-work at the level of the classroom and school and in the public sphere. We must understand and address the social, political, and historical factors that are shaping the current educational landscape in order to persuasively make the argument for microexchanges to inform macrolevel polices. Organizing campaigns are presented as our best hope for changing the discourse and policies that will allow for the conditions to implement pedagogical approaches that will lead to significant and sustainable improvements in student learning. This book offers suggestions for creating spaces where identity-work can occur and how to devise constructive language and models to approach this work in our diverse and quickly changing world.

CHAPTER 2

Getting a View of Students and Teachers in the School Reform Picture

Who students are influences how they interact, respond, and learn in class-rooms. That is, the experiences they have had in their families, their previous experiences with institutions such as schools, as well as the larger social and political frameworks in which they have operated, have shaped their class-room interaction. In turn, who they are as individuals in terms of race, gender, and class contributes to classroom interactions.

—S. J. McCarthey and E. B. Moje (2002, p. 229)

There has been a plethora of new models and improvement strategies for schools and teaching during the past 50 years in American education (Ravitch, 2011) and perhaps an even greater number of fads and educational movements (e.g., open classrooms, whole language, back-to-basics) in urban schools, particularly during the 1980s and 1990s (Payne, 2008). Much of this experimentation culminated in the passage of No Child Left Behind in 2001, a federal bill that supported free-market models and advocated for accountability, choice, and standards as the lever to create national improvement (Belfield & Levin, 2009).

Free-market strategies, such as vouchers, charter schools, and private educational management organizations, rest upon the idea that providing educational choice will spur innovation and produce better educational options while forcing failing schools to close. While NCLB has garnered debate and controversy on several levels (e.g., the lack of additional resources, the variety of rigor in standards and assessments by states), the law continues to shape policy debates. Due to critiques waged by educational researchers, practitioners, and the larger public, the federal Department of Education has pivoted away from following NCLB as it was signed into law. The NCLB Act was passed in 2001 during the George W. Bush administration as the reauthorization of the Elementary and Secondary Education Act (ESEA); it was designed to ensure all K–12 schools met the same standards while increasing educational choice for parents. This legislation articulated policies around accountability and assessment, teacher quality, budget, choice and charters, and supplemental educational services, among other areas of education.

The difficulty of gaining enough support in Congress to pass the reauthorization of the ESEA or NCLB, which expired in 2007, led to an invitation for states to apply for waivers to bypass some of NCLB's onerous reporting requirements and interventions—46 states elected to do so. The waiver program was the Obama administration's way of working around the congressional stalemate and putting forward a new education platform. NCLB had placed a spotlight on school reform and highlighted both problems and inequities in the nation's public education system. In the wake of NCLB, new reforms have been introduced, the most prominent being the Common Core State Standards developed by the Governors Association and the Council of Chief State School Officers. The Obama administration has advocated strongly for the Common Core, which standardizes English and math curricula across states and seeks to ensure that students are prepared for college and careers upon graduation. States were given the choice whether they wanted to implement the CCSS but were incentivized to do so through Race to the Top, a 4 billion dollar grant that assigned higher points to proposals that included the adoption of CCSS. It was imagined that these standards would open the door to more teacher freedom in the classroom, freed as they are from the rote requirements and the focus on testing. However, the Common Core, as I argue, introduces a new set of challenges and limitations that are likely to hamper teachers' abilities to capitalize on identity-making as a tool to engage students. Despite the admission that federal policies such as NCLB were flawed from the start (Orfield, 2009), more recent reforms—NCLB waivers and the Common Core State Standards—do not correct the rigid prescriptions for instructional practice and the narrow definitions of student learning that they were expected to remedy (Karp, 2013; Polikoff, McEachin, Wrabel, & Duque, 2014).

A number of educational researchers have argued that urban school reform is designed to fail for a host of reasons, including the focus on policy gimmicks like vouchers, charters, and tests (Noguera, 2003), a discourse of color-blindness (Fine, 1991; Pollock, 2005), or simply devaluing the capacities and worth of the students. Lipman (2011) suggests that policies must move the "condition of students of color and other marginalized groups to the center of discussions about school restructuring" (pp. 17, 19). Payne attributes the intransigency of school improvement to the fact that "the social dimensions of the problem are still almost certainly the least appreciated" (2008, p. 6).

I agree with these arguments, particularly the fact that education reform and school improvement efforts such as NCLB often fall short of the goal to provide a high-quality education for all because they fail to recognize the social dimensions of the existing barriers. It is impossible to produce improved learning outcomes unless the identities that teachers and learners bring, and the way they shape the school and classroom culture, are a consideration of the reform strategy. In drawing on the experiences of two classroom teachers, this book illuminates the inextricable link between social identities and student learning and provides a glimpse into why any attempts to change instruction and improve student learning must take a holistic account of the teacher and the learner.

Andrea, a classroom teacher who serves as a central case study, articulated this point, drawing a clear link between self-reflection, improving instructional practice, developing students, and making larger societal change:

> You know, I teach for change; I don't see how people who are really teaching for change, for a positive change, cannot take a look at who they are . . . you deepen that layer, and we need to go deeper if we're really going to build this country and make it what it really should be. (personal communication, November 10, 2005)

To begin with a goal of creating systemic improvement for students served by urban educational systems, we must understand the challenging process of creating change, and we must also understand that the process of identity-making among youth and adults is a central feature of this work. I advance these propositions here by arguing that we need to account for the background of teachers and learners and the social dynamics of schooling; interactions among educators, between teachers and families, and between peers are key to improvement efforts. Educational policies are designed to fail because they identify student failure as the fundamental problem and link poor student outcomes solely to race and poverty. If policymakers believe that teachers' capacities or qualifications are the reason for poor student performance in urban schools, then the policies will continue to de-professionalize rather than provide the support and school-based development that have been shown to increase teacher efficacy and change teacher practice (Darling-Hammond, 1997). The importance of creating a professional collaborative culture has been established as a vehicle to support teacher learning and to provide spaces where teachers can receive collegial support when developing new instructional strategies (DuFour, 2004).

My research revealed that teachers yearn for embedded professional development opportunities that are crucial to creating reflective practice and pedagogical change. A small group of teachers in a multiracial cross-school study group that I facilitated expressed an interest in having more time to process teaching moments, more time to discuss practices with their colleagues, and additional opportunities to challenge beliefs about who their students were while they interrogated beliefs about the self. One of the teachers, Ellen, said, "We are so desperate for this kind of professional development. When we had those talks about individual students, it changed the way that we saw our kids" (personal communication, February 24, 2007).

This type of professional learning is exactly what is required to improve teaching; a different view of students—an understanding of their lives and what motivates them—is necessary. Teachers cannot reverse current academic trends until policies allow for educators to bring their whole selves and their professional judgment to bear in teaching decisions. In addition, rather than continuing to rig the system against students while blaming them for failure, we must value students' culture, document their resilience, and present them with better resourced schools as well as challenging curricula that will capture their interests and open up a variety of future opportunities.

WHY IDENTITIES OF TEACHERS MATTER IN SCHOOL IMPROVEMENT

Facilitating a cross-school study group and conducting teacher life histories and year-end interviews with six classroom teachers allowed me to trace how the interactions between teachers and students inform the identity-making of both. At the same time, I documented how social identities influenced pedagogical decisions and student goals. I used life history interviews to establish connections between teacher identity and personal belief systems and linked these factors to decisionmaking. The beliefs that teachers held regarding instructing across differences, whether it was viewed as an affordance or a constraint, have bearing on how they interact with students as well as on their pedagogy. The group of teachers who participated in the study group understood that their identities informed what happened in the classroom and tended to use two central mechanisms for leveraging student identities: the content of a curriculum or the structure of a classroom (e.g., the design of participation strategies). These examples demonstrated how identities mediate teacher and student behaviors and, in turn, the teaching and learning process.

While I focus on only two portraits (out of six cases), the philosophies teachers expressed about how to create successful learners underscored the importance of teachers knowing the learners, loving their content area, using multiple strategies to help students develop a deeper understanding and use their talents to contribute to the classroom and the world, while designing a safe learning environment in which students can take risks. Most of these teachers saw developing a student's identity as a significant part of their responsibilities as classroom teachers. Yet, creating space for this was frequently thwarted by the administration of benchmark and statewide assessments. As I show, Ellen and Andrea approached teaching in different ways, but each brought her identity as a mentor, a political actor, a content area expert, and a reflective practitioner into the classroom. Ellen, for example, believes deeply in math as a path to future success, and her own life experiences have contributed to her desire to show her students how far education can take them. That means, as I'll show, doing more than teaching to standardized assessments.

When teachers talked about developing their students' identities, they were referring to helping students build a sense of self, developing confidence, evaluating their behavior and choices, and examining the self in relation to society. Some of this work happened through the relationships that were built between the teacher and student, some of it occurred through teacher modeling, and in a few cases it was directly tied to the curriculum.

TWO TEACHER PORTRAITS

I selected Dr. Ellen Clay and Ms. Andrea Carter as central examples because in addition to life history and year-end interviews and study group conversations with the two, I was a participant–observer in their classrooms 2 days per week over the course of an academic year. These teachers were, in fact, the individuals at each school whom I first approached to participate in my study, and at that time I inquired whether I could visit their classroom several times a week.

Ellen brings an intense energy to everything she does. She is outgoing and direct about her thoughts and feelings, a quality that seems to catch some people off guard. She is a White woman who was in her mid-forties during the time of the study. She was raised in a small, segregated working- and middle-class community in the rural South. She started teaching middle school after earning a PhD in mathematics and teaching at the university level for more than a decade. While for the first part of her professional career, she identified as a mathematician, she now sees herself as an educator working for social change, someone who uses math as a vehicle to grant young people greater educational access.

In the small town where she grew up people typically attended the same elementary school and high school. There were two major options available to students who decided to attend college, both of them public state colleges. During the 9 years that Ellen spent at the local university earning her BA and PhD, she learned that there were a variety of ways to look at things, and all was not as simple as had been presented to her by her family and community. The town was divided spatially by race, and it was not until her graduate studies that she began to understand issues of race, class, and gender discrimination due to her previously limited interaction with and discussion about people from different backgrounds. She describes these years of study as difficult, times that forced her to mature and shed many of the lessons that her family and culture had instilled in her.

Ellen believes that justice is the most important human value. "That's what drives me: I want my kids, my students, to have every opportunity available, and it's, you know, it's clear that I can't make that happen, but for some of them I can begin to make that happen" (personal communication, October 27, 2005). Put simply, Ellen would like to have every student who leaves her middle school math class complete the year on grade level no matter where they started out. For students who are particularly bright, the goal is to "teach them as far as they can go" even if it is 9th-grade material. It is her belief that math can open up opportunities, but more important, it is also the primary gatekeeper that impedes future choices such as high school enrollment, course taking, and college attendance. This fact motivates her to make up lost ground for students, find ways to turn students on to math, and in general to teach her middle school students enough so that they will have the confidence to take on calculus and complete high school, regardless of the quality of the teacher to whom they are assigned.

Andrea, a humanities teacher, is an African American woman who was in her early thirties. She grew up in a working-poor family in a northeast city. Although she had been teaching for 7 years, by all appearances it seemed she had been at this work for far longer. Having grown up in the same city where she now teaches, Andrea identifies strongly with her students because she sees the experiences of their childhood as closely mirroring her own. The primary reason Andrea is in the classroom is to develop students' knowledge so they will make good choices. Teaching represents an opportunity for her to make a difference in the lives of her students, whom she considers her extended community.

Andrea and her six sisters were raised by their mother, and while Andrea describes her childhood as happy and carefree, she acknowledges that she was unaware of the struggles (financial and personal) her mother faced. Andrea's family background is similar to her students', but her educational background stands in contrast to theirs. She was sent to a Catholic school first, and then went off to a small private boarding school outside of the city. After finishing near the top of her class, she enrolled at a comprehensive public research university. In her first year, she became pregnant, which she hid for 6 months out of surprise and shame. Andrea dedicated herself to finding a way to continue with college and care for her daughter. She took one month off during the spring semester when she delivered the baby and then was able to catch up and complete her 1st year of college. After a year on public assistance, she resolved to do anything she needed to do to support herself and her child while finishing school. She worked through college and still managed to finish in 4 years. Her college graduation, with her daughter in attendance, was a high point in her adult life, she says. She enrolled directly in a master's program in teaching, and soon after she started teaching in urban elementary schools.

Andrea's main goal is to develop students' knowledge so they can make good choices. Teaching represents an opportunity for her to make a difference in youths' lives, her extended community. She recognizes that if it were not for her teachers and the strength of her mother, who helped her develop independent thinking, she might have ended up living in a public housing project. The choices she has made over the course of her life have positioned her in such a way that she can make a difference in the lives of her students and the broader community. As she says, "I teach so that my kids can have choices and that they'll have the knowledge to make the right choices . . . and that goes back to teaching for understanding, so they understand the ways of the world, and with their reading and with understanding enough to write and articulate [their ideas] they'll be able to make better choices in life" (personal communication, February 8, 2006). Andrea would like students to understand that things happen because of the choices people make. One does not have to be in her classroom for long to recognize that her passion and her intensity are fueled by her desire to see students learn and achieve.

The work around developing students' sense of self is explicit in Andrea's classroom. She intentionally stands as a model for what they can become, but her story alone does not stand as a representation of the goal; she also consistently demonstrates what to do and be, how to express feelings, and how to articulate or record ideas. Andrea's sense that writing comes from within supports the important work of students' identity development. In every single composition that students craft, they share a piece of themselves. In addition, she models behaviors that demonstrate readiness for learning, strategies that lead to effective readers, writers, and thinkers. She believes that teachers "add to the [student] culture in such a big way. We really do determine what kind of person they may become" (personal communication, June 12, 2006).

Connecting Identity Portraits to Belief Systems

These teacher portraits begin to reveal how individuals' experiences inform identities, beliefs, and actions. Identity-work is complicated and constantly evolving, which makes drawing a definitive relationship between identities, beliefs, and actions difficult. Despite the complexity of such processes, interesting patterns emerged in the group of teachers who participated in the cross-school study group. For example, three of the teachers raised daughters on their own while they were in the process of getting their bachelor's degrees, which points to a firm belief in the value of higher education. The power of mentors was a recurring theme, one that was based on their own relationships with early mentors. They also shared beliefs about the elements of the teacher role but diverged on their views of what it meant to teach across difference.

In the larger group of participating teachers, the question about whether to recognize the difference in individuals' backgrounds in efforts to create greater equity surfaced during the first and final session. In the life history interviews, teachers talked about feeling different from others, feeling marginalized by society, and wanting people, structures, and institutions to be more equitable. It was surprising to discover that during their childhood or young adulthood, all of the teachers in the cross-school study group were in a minority group in their home community in terms of religion (1 person), class (3), gender (1), or race (3). I suspect that these identities, with one exception, are deeply connected to their beliefs about equity and have prompted them to see the value in the diversity of human experiences. For the purpose of providing concrete cases that are informed by and should inform education policy, I report on two focal teachers.

Ellen's childhood context and social status allowed her fewer opportunities to develop the tools and knowledge necessary to work toward her goal of creating more equitable social conditions. While both Ellen and Andrea experienced life and pursued paths filled with various obstacles, Ellen recognizes her good fortune given the stable and supportive home environment in which she was raised. There were no major struggles at home, "no alcoholism, no abuse, no nothing . . . and no understanding that there was racism, gender discrimination, class [discrimination], nothing" (personal communication, October 27, 2005). One piece of her identity that informs her current philosophy is being an individual who had to unlearn and relearn all that she had come to know in the first 26 years of life. In identifying a central theme that connected her life history, Ellen stated, "My life is about learning, and transforming, and worrying about how much I have left to learn" (personal communication, October 27, 2005).

The sense of reflection, learning, and change are common to both Ellen's and Andrea's stories, but because of her positionality, Ellen has a palpable sense of urgency behind her commitment to educating students of color and students from lower socioeconomic backgrounds. Despite the fact that she was not exposed to more diverse contexts until well into her twenties, at her school and in her classroom Ellen consistently spoke up about difference, stereotypes, and inequitable school practices (e.g., ability grouping). This is noteworthy given a recent social trend in the United States heralding "color blindness," a belief that it is better to ignore and silence representations of difference (Crenshaw, Gotanda, Peller, & Thomas, 1995). This phenomenon is particularly common in schools where racial identifications are erased from public talk but not necessarily from people's consciousness and frameworks about achievement (Pollock, 2001).

Like Ellen, Andrea sees teaching as a way to change the world. She views her role as a literacy instructor as one that provides students with tools to examine themselves and society at large. Her vision of education explicitly connects her content area with issues of equity and social justice.

> I see the potential in our people becoming educated about how we can change the face of the world. I think I'm genuine and I'm real . . . so I often share part of myself with them, and my beliefs. I let them know that I believe in you, I know that you are a child of color. I know that life for you was different than the vast majority, but you can make a

difference. Okay, things can change, and that change needs to start with you. . . . I try to let them know that I am always reading the world and my views of the world may change, but ultimately it changes because of who I become. (personal communication, April 1, 2005)

Her use of "our" indicates that she is speaking of a shared community of which she and her students are a part. While each individual might come from a different background, she imagines that as people of color in the world, there is a commonality that binds them.

Andrea recounts a memorable experience in high school that sheds light on her family background and the development of her pedagogical stance. A classmate of hers, Andrew, had an aggressive outburst during her sophomore English class challenging her favorite teacher about the content of the texts and the fact that all of the authors in their curriculum were White. When the teacher tried to calm Andrew down by pointing out that the sacrifices and leadership of the country's founders and foremost intellectuals must be acknowledged, Andrea remembered thinking the teacher was right. She also remembers thinking, "What is wrong with Andrew?" (personal communication, February 8, 2006). During college, she began to read and learn more about Black people and their experiences in America. This knowledge shifted Andrea's sense of herself in the world and made her committed to educating young students and presenting a fuller version of American history.

Years later, she reflected on this incident and wished for the opportunity to have a rich conversation with Andrew about education and the world. She also imagined commending his father on the important lessons he had imparted to his son. This stood out because Andrea's mother raised her not to question or to "make trouble." Her mother had been brought up to do what was expected of her, and as a result of this "home training" in her early years, Andrea tended not to challenge the status quo.

Andrea's memories of the incident with Andrew and her own upbringing connect back to her vision about "people becoming educated about how we can change the face of the world" (personal communication, April 1, 2005). Andrea models a reflective stance for her students in a way that informs their social development, but it is also part and parcel of much of their academic work. This pedagogical approach requires students to reflect on who they are as individuals and to examine this openly with her and their peers. Andrea's openness allows her students to be themselves, so that their identities (and hers) become a critical part of the educational process.

This process unfolded in a variety of ways in her classroom. After Andrea had the class read bell hooks' *Skin Again* (2009), she asked students to reflect on what the book was about and if it lined up with the predictions that they had made prior to reading the text. She read a phrase from the text, "Come look at the inside, not just outside," and asked students what words hooks used to describe the inside of a person. This literacy lesson came to a close by Andrea informing students that they should practice looking deep inside people rather than making quick judgments based on outward appearances.

Connecting Identities and Beliefs to Teacher Goals

Andrea and Ellen share the goal of exposing students to rigorous curricula in an effort to ensure success in school and increase the likelihood that students will take college preparatory courses and later enroll in college. They are able to succeed with students in part because both are reflective practitioners who participate in a variety of teacher learning networks. They both seek out spaces where they can talk about their practice, learn about current educational research, and share their knowledge as well as their teaching dilemmas. Both also call on additional supports and experts to enrich the curriculum and provide mentorship to their students. Like other successful teachers, they are masters at pulling in resources to support their students' academic growth.

Another factor that contributes to their ability to make significant academic progress with students is the consistent teacher-based assessment of students' learning that allows them to identify when students need more help. These ongoing formative assessments diverged from the current frames for thinking about assessment. They were integrated into classroom activities and provided much richer information to inform teaching and the needs of individual students than district-generated benchmarks. In many instances, they made midcourse corrections when students reached stumbling blocks by retooling a lesson or individualizing instruction so that students develop a deep understanding of the content. In making these midcourse corrections, they attempt to ensure that students are making the knowledge their own.

Despite these similarities, there are also differences in their teaching philosophies and practices. These differences can be connected to the content area they teach, the grade level, or, more fundamentally, to how they see their role as teacher. In study group discussions, there was an ongoing debate about the feasibility of getting to know students and the ways in which teachers could reveal their background and beliefs in the process of teaching math. One math teacher who taught 5th grade believed that there was space to connect the math curriculum to students' lives. She suspected that if you did not build on students' lives and interests outside of school, they would have less success in developing math knowledge.

At the beginning of the year we talked about "our memorable math moment" and some of them would say they didn't like math, they were failing math. I had quite a few students who had that outlook on mathematics. But I would sit down with them and just talk about what they did do well, and validating it. And saying . . . I think one of the good things about teaching mathematics is that you might stink in one thing, but you could be excellent in another area. I think just validating what they could do, and making them feel like that was worth something. (personal communication, July 1, 2006)

Ellen went back and forth about whether it was perhaps more difficult to make math relevant and engage students that way. There was more space to examine social issues when she taught social studies to middle school students in her first secondary school assignment. While subject area undoubtedly informs teaching goals and practices, I have primarily focused on how teachers and students construct identities independent of a particular content area. Drake, Spillane, and Hufferd-Ackles (2001) have argued that the stories teachers construct relative to their identities vary greatly from one subject area to another.

Contextual Factors That Inform Teachers' Beliefs

Teachers' philosophical orientations are informed not only by their background and identities but also by the students they teach. The institutional culture and classroom environment have a great deal to do with how teaching philosophies change and develop over time. Teachers actively resisted dominant and institutional framings of urban students (not smart, limited future, no assets in community or home), but Ellen and Andrea also adopted definitions held by mainstream society in an effort to make sense of the challenging circumstances they confronted. It seems from the following examples that the inconsistencies that surfaced in their stance and philosophies were tied to the challenge of producing student success in the school and classroom contexts in which they were situated. McAdams (1993) suggests that stories define who we are. His theory on human identity is framed on the idea that "each of us comes to know who he or she is by creating a heroic story of self" (p. 11). In an effort to make sense of themselves and preserve a sense of goodness and integrity, Ellen and Andrea occasionally had to devise rationales when they blamed students, gave up on an individual pupil, or applied a strategy they might ordinarily reject.

Ellen, who talked about her impatience getting in the way of doing whatever it takes to reach a student, provides an example of a no-win scenario in her first K–12 teaching assignment at an urban charter school.

There was a kid there who was, you know, a foot taller than me, a big guy, and you know, I taught him math every day, and he was a very troubled kid. His mother was in a wheelchair, maybe had MS or something, a [degenerative] disease, and he was a very angry kid, and he had issues with me. So one day in the cafeteria, he yelled across the cafeteria at me . . . "You White bitch!" And I don't really know what to do with this, so I go back to the classroom, whatever, and I tell the disciplinarian. I really don't know what to do. Well, if I suspend him, because clearly this is a "suspendable " offense, he's going back to juvenile detention. He's 14 and he'll be there till he's 18. I'm not trained in this. I have visions of what "juvee" must look like . . . and I decide I'm not qualified to make this decision. So [the disciplinarian] decides that he won't suspend him, and then I'm thinking the next morning, obviously crying, what am I going to do with him in my class? (personal communication, October 21, 2005)

This event demonstrates the challenging circumstances in which students and teachers may find themselves. Suspending the student would intensify the challenges he already faced, but allowing him to participate in the classroom after this incident did not serve the young man, Ellen, or the class as a whole. She was devastated by the exchange and came to view the student as a real threat to her personal safety. In an effort to be fair to the student, she went along with the administrator's decision not to suspend him, but just a few weeks later the student broke curfew and returned to the juvenile justice system.

This experience certainly influenced her beliefs about urban students, particularly because this experience was among her first encounters with children of color from a large city. She chose to teach in this environment because she wanted to learn more about the student populations she would encounter, but inevitably she would draw on stereotypical models of Black males as dangerous and criminal (Ferguson, 2001), frameworks that may have gained validity in Ellen's mind because of this interaction.

Despite a commitment to working against identifications that serve as barriers to students' success, when caught in a bind, teachers can succumb to definitions held by the wider society. Another example of this was the class of 2005–2006 at Andrea's school. Teachers and administrators viewed the entire class as low-level learners; this led Andrea to believe that students were let down and not given the opportunity to achieve in their previous educational contexts. She struggled to dislodge the identities her students were assigned, first by building individual relationships, and then by talking with them about how they saw themselves. She imparted her philosophy that "we all have challenges, we all have strengths that can help us overcome some of our challenges" (personal communication, July 26, 2006).

Andrea held a strong belief that this group of students could be successful, and over the course of the year, she was able to see significant academic and personal growth in each child. Even when students fell short of her standards, she understood this to mean that they had not given the work their complete effort rather than believing they were incapable of it. One morning, when students failed to hand in a long-term assignment, she was "disappointed," she told me, "because students are lazy . . . it is very disappointing all the time you put, in all the supports students receive. It is not that they can't do it; they have just decided they do not want to" (personal communication, December 6, 2005).

The year I had spent as a participant observer in Andrea's classroom influenced my reading of the interaction. The term *lazy* when applied to Black students has lasting historical implications, used from slavery to contemporary times to provide a rationale for the lowly status and life circumstances. Andrea was making a point to stress that she knew that students were capable and smart—something that they had not been told consistently in the past—yet, at the same time, she applied an adjective that called up a negative sociohistorical model of African American identity. Ironically, this is the exact type of model that Andrea works hard to contest. When I shared this incident and a variety of other classroom interactions with Andrea, she immediately focused on her framing of the problem.

> I have to remind myself that they are still children and that there are going to be those moments and not to take things personal. And just really revisiting what I can do to expedite the process and support them even more because sometimes I think that I'm giving them supports, [but] obviously maybe they haven't been given enough supports and it just calls for me to restructure my thinking. (personal communication, May 23, 2006)

Having an opportunity to reflect on this teaching moment, Andrea was reminded of the importance of considering students' perspectives and generational status. Even though she had provided supports and given students numerous opportunities and reminders to complete their assignments, she admonished herself for not considering that students' actions could suggest that she had not done enough for them.

The ability to reflect on interactions with students in a moment of frustration is what separates average from exceptional teachers—exemplified in Ellen's and Andrea's reflective practice. These examples highlight the importance of considering teacher background, student identities, and the context of not only the school system but also the larger society as factors that inform the teaching and learning process. Teacher participants of the study group were dedicated to taking into account the variety of forces in the complex educational system and at the same time taking responsibility for what they might need to learn about and do differently to engage the students in their particular classrooms.

The importance of teacher identity and beliefs and the role this plays in understanding students' experiences and needs are conveyed through the cases of Ellen and Andrea. We can see how larger sociohistorical structures inform school and classroom practices and also contribute to the design of deficit-based policies that constrain professional decisionmaking and student learning.

Perhaps if educational policymakers believed, as the dedicated urban teachers who participated in this study did, that with the appropriate supports and resources teachers could teach well and students could become advanced, then designs for improvement would be more effective. We must keep in mind that, much like students who feel "schooling" intends to make them different from who they are, it is not entirely different for educators; "the undercurrent of race is never far from the surface, and the new leaders would do well to remember that some members of the community often feel that reform is often *done* to them" (Reville, 2007, p. 34; emphasis in original). This is to say, their expertise, experiences, and needs are not considered in the process of educational change. We must keep in focus the conditions of urban communities and the ways they produce people and organizations (such as schools). To ignore issues of race, class, and power in educational systems necessarily places the blame for failure on students, families, and teachers. Locating the problem in any (or all) of these bodies leads to policies that are founded on a lack of trust, little autonomy, and a denial of agency for the central educational actors.

The next chapter explores how Ellen's and Andrea's life histories and social identities influence teaching decisions, particularly when confronted with new federal, state, and regional mandates that they describe as constraining teaching decisions and bumping up against their pedagogical goals.

CHAPTER 3

Leveraging Teacher Autonomy to Engage Learners

Moving toward standards and accountability as key levers for improving education is a strategy that was conceptualized several decades before the adoption of the No Child Left Behind Act. *A Nation at Risk: The Imperative for Education Reform*, a report authored in 1983 by President Reagan's National Commission on Excellence in Education, initiated a wave of concern about how American students were faring as compared to their counterparts throughout the world. Years later, the No Child Left Behind Act was designed as a direct response to this report, with a focus on the standards, expectations, instructional time, quality of teachers and leaders, and greater fiscal support for education.

Despite the articulated intent of federal policy to ensure access to quality schooling for all children in the nation, many believe that the reform agenda has decreased teachers' autonomy and decisionmaking power and has instead created systems of accountability that tend to jeopardize teachers' work rather than motivate them to improve their practice. Some have argued that the outcome of this federal policy undermines not only student success but also public education on the whole, by weakening schools, imposing impossible requirements, and narrowly defining learning outcomes (Mintrop & Sunderman, 2009). Other educational researchers have suggested that the negative effect high-stakes testing started to have in suburban districts and schools serving middle- and upper-middle-class families was a key turning point where public disapproval and pressure to revise NCLB gained traction (see Karp, 2013).

As a result of these research-based critiques, teacher and parent organizing, and the dismal progress of U.S. schools, particularly those in urban centers, there has been a change of course (or at least in discourse) by the federal government. Arne Duncan, the U.S. Secretary of Education, stated that "the act's emphasis on test scores as the primary measure of school performance has narrowed the curriculum, and the one-size-fits-all accountability system has mislabeled schools as failures even if their students are demonstrating real academic growth" (Duncan, 2012). The Common Core was designed to remedy these pitfalls by providing rigorous curricular goals

24

shared by states that identified learning outcomes for high school graduates that would prepare them well for college or careers. Some educators were hopeful that new frameworks would lead to curricula focused on interdisciplinary learning—critical reading of a variety of texts and a balance between building conceptual mathematical understanding and procedural fluency—and that the decisions about curriculum and assessment tasks would be in the hands of teachers. The possibilities presented by this shift in federal policies make the arguments and recommendations of this book more salient. Creating teacher autonomy and space in the curriculum for identity-work is critical to improving student learning. If we can focus on this goal when designing professional development plans and timelines for implementing accountability measures related to student performance on Common Core performance tasks (assessments), students will be far better served.

The argument that I have made about the relationship between identity-making and learning extends to the nature of curriculum and how it is implemented. Through the classroom examples, I demonstrate that high-interest curricula or flexible, student-centered, classroom participation structures designed to make content relevant to individual students and/or explicitly link to out-of-school applications increase student engagement in the learning process. If students are engaged, they will be active participants in their learning, and this will increase how much they learn and their ability to demonstrate their knowledge. Engagement is not simply students demonstrating that they are invested in academic work through participation and the completion of tasks, but instead it should be understood as the dialectical relationship between student and teacher, as well as between curriculum and individual; it is a process of democratic participation in a community (McMahon & Portelli, 2004). If we want to improve students' educational experiences and future opportunities, then students must be engaged in learning that they deem meaningful.

Learning, like identity construction, is dialectical, and if equal emphasis is placed on the learners' background, interests, and experiences out of school as academic learning, not only will it improve student outcomes, but it will also develop successful and agentive individuals—citizens with an ability to critique their educational experiences and society more broadly (Westheimer & Kahne, 1998). If teaching and learning are intertwined with the identities of the teacher and the learner, then the implementation of curriculum is a key space for identity-work. The importance of creating intellectual engagement and inquiry is related not only to students' learning but also to students' views of self. This process is mutually reinforcing—if students see themselves as active participants in their learning who are capable of achieving, not only will they be more successful, but they are more likely to push for the resources and supports they need to excel (Oakes & Rogers, 2006).

Even skeptics who continue to see identity construction as peripheral to the role of the classroom teacher might concede that engaging the learner is a first step toward improving learning outcomes. So, if we seek to engage learners, it is imperative that we present a curriculum that is of high interest and relevant to students' lives. Teachers who are oriented toward making learning relevant identify openings in their fairly prescriptive curriculum to implement pedagogical decisions that will draw students into academic work. That is to say, in order to innovate, practitioners need to "teach for openings" (Greene, 1995, p. 109). This becomes more challenging in a context where constantly changing reforms detract from teachers' focus on developing a personal instructional style and integrating new standards, curricula, and assessments into their pedagogical plan

The focal teachers, like many of their colleagues, made use of the autonomy afforded them, whether it is officially granted due to the type of school (university partnership school, pilot school, or charter school) or the school's status in relation to others in the district. Individual teachers might "earn" teaching autonomy as a result of credentials, their reputation in the educational community, or successes measured by student performance, test scores, or students' acceptance to selective high schools or colleges.

Ellen and Andrea, who are highlighted in the following examples, maintain more autonomy than the average teacher in their schools and certainly when compared with others in the large urban school district where they were employed. They experienced a fair amount of flexibility because the schools where they taught attained adequate yearly progress, meaning the schools met requirements of the federal NCLB Act. They also had more autonomy because the classes of students they taught during the previous year had made significant progress relative to the teachers' professional learning standards as well as state assessments.

These examples are presented to demonstrate what is possible when teachers have autonomy and are committed to using curricular content or participation structures to engage learners. While I am not arguing that every teacher will meet the same success, I do mean to suggest that the more autonomy and professional support teachers are afforded, the greater the likelihood of deepening relationships and increasing academic success. Committed teachers who experience real constraints around curriculum and more punitive accountability structures can still engage in identity-work through their teaching stance—one that foregrounds inquiry (Cochran-Smith, 2004; Cochran-Smith & Lytle, 2009), listening (Schultz, 2003), and affirming difference (Nieto, 1996). Over the past decade, improving public schools, teaching practice, and student performance has been framed as a technical or efficiency issue rather than a learning problem; this framing makes identity-work more difficult to accomplish because it is seen as peripheral to teaching and learning. Teachers who bend the rules by ignoring or altering mandates in order to make professional decisions that they deem are in the best interest of their students often do so at great risk. They surmise that their students' engagement, learning, and future success are more important than the potential consequence of these choices.

ENGAGING LEARNERS THROUGH CURRICULAR ADAPTATIONS

The process of exploring and unpacking teachers' curricular decisions involves much more than the content area and delivery of curricula. I have also chosen to focus on teaching decisions such as how information is presented and how informal learning is addressed and incorporated into the classroom (or not) as well as curricular units and out-of-school trips. When we think about a curriculum as an opportunity to engage in identity-making, examining students' responses to and interactions with the curriculum presented and how teachers insert a range of topics that are not represented in the formal curriculum becomes particularly instructive.

Adolescent learners rarely find intrinsic interest or extrinsic benefit through the study of a content area, for example, learning the logic of mathematics (Newman, 1989). Instead, teachers must develop a variety of tactics to "hook" students (Bruner, 1960), or draw them into learning, whether focusing on extrinsic rewards (e.g., good grades, trips, public praise, candy) or developing internally derived motivation (e.g., acquiring new knowledge, understanding self and community, contributing to society, or becoming agents of change).

A technique that Ellen Clay used to motivate and engage her 7th-grade students was sharing with them the fact that the math she was presenting was 8th- or 9th-grade material. She also reminded her class that their scores on tests would be their gateway to the high school of their choice. This was connected to her certainty that if students wanted to learn, she could teach them anything. She believed that most students in this class would work even harder when presented with the fact that they were being given work 1 or 2 years above their grade level. This strategy did, in fact, keep the class of students, who were the "highest-track" group in 7th grade, focused on learning.

One student, Randy, who was described by several teachers as a difficult student who was hard to engage, stated:

> My teacher ... she sometimes might go by the book and do stuff that's in the book. But if she get a lesson that she think won't benefit us ... she won't let us do that. Like, we was working on the algebra, doing, like, 10th- and 11th-grade stuff. She said that was going to help us in the future ... so I like doing that. (R. Tobin, personal communication, May 4, 2006)

Another way that Ellen sought to engage her students was through a local historical data project designed to connect the math curriculum with students' lives as residents of a particular community. The project allowed students to interact with primary source documents from the early 20th century and craft research based upon interesting patterns in census data. The students were in effect learning math skills while studying a topic that might be construed as unrelated to mathematics.

Andrea had her own way of motivating and engaging her 5th-grade students. Over the course of the year, Andrea presented at least three major curriculum units as a vehicle for learning about history and literature while developing reading and writing skills. Those units were the Harlem Renaissance, I-search essays, and I-movies (a culminating year-end activity in which students use multimedia, such as photos, audio, and editing software, to create a digital story about some aspect of their lives). These projects were nontraditional, and each could serve as a cohesive example to unpack the types of curricular choices that Andrea made while at the same time allowing for an examination of the issues that motivated such decisions. While research projects are new and challenging terrain for elementary students, they are a common feature of 5th-grade curricula. In the next two sections I take a closer look at projects each teacher presented in an effort to engage learners through connecting to their interests and backgrounds.

The examples that follow point to the ways that teachers' previous successes (as measured by the performance of former students) led to more teaching autonomy; this allowed Ellen and Andrea to adapt and supplement the standard curriculum to better meet student needs. While some teachers may need more supports (human resources, professional development, instructional modeling) in order to implement similar curricular units, all teachers should have the space to teach with interdisciplinary project-based units that connect to students' identities because we know it leads to increased engagement and more powerful learning.

Historical Data Analysis Project

At the end of February, during a time of intense preparation for statewide assessments, math students in Ellen's classroom spent a few weeks on practice tests, first working independently and then in groups. One class period began with students looking at their work and making corrections before handing in their tests to Ellen. While students reviewed their assignment, Ellen took an opportunity to talk to them about an upcoming project she was considering and to explain the presence of a visitor who had come to their classroom earlier that day.

Ellen was herself enrolled in a history class for teachers at a nearby university. The course allowed teachers to make use of local historical resources to develop a hands-on project. Ellen informed the class that the gentleman who visited was a historian and the instructor of her graduate school course. She asked students whether they would be interested in studying their city blocks and learning about their neighborhood around the time of the early 20th century. They responded very enthusiastically. Randy made a point of saying that he wanted to look at blocks in his neighborhood; he chanted the name of his street over and over. Ellen therefore decided that the class would take on the project, and she informed students of this decision before she continued with what she had planned for that class period (fieldnotes, February 24, 2006).

Developing and carrying out this data analysis unit required as much history content and social science research as math and representation skills. *The Philadelphia Negro* (DuBois, 1899) was used as an introduction to the type of data collection methods and research that students would undertake. After becoming familiar with the types of questions that are researchable and the various ways to represent data in tables, charts, and graphs, the class went on a neighborhood walk. In each of the groups, students were armed with GIS maps (computerized database for storing, retrieving, analyzing, and displaying spatial data) and clipboards; they recorded which buildings were still in existence and what changes had occurred on their assigned blocks.

Although it was logistically impossible to have each student study his or her own block, they were able to learn about the properties and inhabitants of nearby blocks, viewing friends' homes and establishments owned by their classmates' families while also noting physical changes in their immediate neighborhood. Students gained the skills of learning to read census data, importing data into Excel charts, identifying meaningful research questions, and making claims about a set of data. If the student researchers discovered that their data set would not provide enough information to address their initial question, they were able to reframe the research inquiry. A range of questions were constructed, such as "How did the occupation of an individual relate to his or her age?" "How did the racial demographics of a block change over time?" "Is the block studied representative of the city in terms of race, gender, occupation, and age?" (E. Clay, personal communication, March 24, 2006). The work culminated in a celebration; parents were invited for lunch in order to view a presentation of students' projects in a poster session.

While Ellen often relied on the structure of her math classroom to engage students in acquiring math knowledge, the goal of this project was to introduce students to data analysis and representation through a community-based project that was relevant to their lives. It was an example of a curriculum being tailored to involve students through building connections to something familiar (their neighborhood) or something of interest (sociological patterns related to race, gender, education, or age).

Ellen confessed that given the data project's length and intensity, in addition to the fact that it only allowed students to work with categorical data, she would have abandoned the project before it was completed if it had occurred prior to the state assessment. Although Ellen, a teacher with relative autonomy, might have cut the project short, there are many teachers who have forgone this type of hands-on project-based work entirely. One of her goals for the unit was to teach statistical analysis through the project, but due to the nature of the type of census data and questions that students posed, this was not actualized.

> If it was a project I started earlier in the semester, I would have figured out a way to wrap it up and end it early because they would not have learned enough math content. For example, all of the data was categorical, not numeric, so there was less they could do in terms of data analysis related to math concepts. (personal communication, June 11, 2006)

The pressure from school administrators and district officials to focus on preparing for state assessments meant that teachers were less likely to implement instructional approaches that were innovative and interdisciplinary. Sometimes teachers waited until after these exams, in April or May, to present project-based work or other curriculum units that could be described as "fun," which often meant high-interest or engaging. In certain school contexts, if we wait until eight months of teaching to present curricula that might captivate students, most students will already be disengaged.

Ellen decided to gauge student interest in the project and give students the option to finish their work, extend their investigation, or stop the project on that very day. Six students in the class indicated that they wanted to finish the project that day, a group of five students wanted to combine their data with another group to create a larger data set, and four students indicated that they wanted to dig deeper and be given a significant amount of additional time to complete their work. Although Ellen felt that this project dragged on and did not allow her to introduce statistical analysis, the majority of students wanted to dig deeper or collaborate further and this opportunity might have been lost because of the pressure of standardized assessments. The opportunity to pose sociological questions about the history of their community, to work collaboratively, and represent data in a variety of formats would have been forfeited. Although this work is arguably not central to the mathematics curriculum, it represented an important moment where identity-work was tied to the official curriculum.

Student interviews provided a different type of evidence for the mixed nature of students' experiences with this data project; of the five students who were interviewed, two identified reading and recording data as new skills they had acquired, two students did not mention the project at all, and one felt he had not learned anything valuable from the study.

Presenting these findings is not intended to minimize the value of project-based learning that connects to students' communities but to raise the possibility that other factors —learning material beyond the 7th-grade level, performing well on tests, and getting high grades—were enough to engage "a really bright class" of students, as Ellen described them. It is also possible that students understood the data project as lower-stakes work and saw it as an opportunity to relax a bit at the close of the year when state assessments were behind them. If teachers did not experience pressure from state assessments or Core Standards tasks, more project-based work would occur over the course of the academic year and would be staggered among the different content areas rather than occurring at the same time in every content area, as was the case for this group of middle school students.

Randy was asked in an interview after this project what he had learned, and he replied, "Well, of course I learned something, like, [did I] learn something that really benefited me? I'm not sure" (personal communication, May 4, 2006). Randy was aware that his teacher made curricular decisions with students in mind, but he was suspicious about the applicability of skills learned during the historical data project, unlike the introduction to algebra unit, which he understood he would use in high school and college.

Harlem Renaissance Unit

The Harlem Renaissance unit, initiated in Andrea Carter's classroom in the beginning of April, also took place after the students completed a week of state exam testing. This was the second research project undertaken in her classroom during the year. The culminating project for this unit was the composition of a biographical essay of one of the key figures of the Harlem Renaissance. Students selected whom they would research based upon their individual interests and then spent 3 weeks developing their research skills and formulating answers to their questions. This experience served as an example for how to explore a new subject. Under Andrea's guidance, the student teacher met with students both as a group and individually to check on the appropriateness of the research materials and their overall progress.

As an additional assignment to the biographical essay for the unit, students responded in writing to the sentence starter, "If I lived in Harlem during the 1920s . . ." Andrea explained that the fictional writing assignment should be informed by what they had learned from their research projects related to the Harlem Renaissance, and she encouraged them to explore the topic in a direction that spoke to their curiosity. At the end of one writing period, she shared two writing samples from students in her other class; one student talked about depicting the world through her artwork, using Aaron Douglass as a role model for the type of art she would like to produce, and another said that he would work in a factory and express his African American identity through music (fieldnotes, April 25, 2006).

On the final day that students had to work on a fictional essay as part of the Harlem Renaissance Unit, Andrea informed her students that they would have 5 minutes to finish their writing and then she would collect and grade their assignment. During the writing period, Andrea took out a small notebook in which she often composed while students were working on their assignments. This is a common practice of the National Writing Project, an initiative that encourages teachers to keep journals so that they are in the practice of composing regularly, just as their students are taught to do. Additionally, instructors are able to model the habit of writing and can share actual examples of their work with students. Andrea read the following entry aloud to her students:

> If I lived in Harlem during the 1920s, I would have taken part in the Harlem Renaissance by writing. I would have been inspired by some of the great writers like Langston Hughes, Countee Cullen, and especially W.E.B. Dubois. Dubois would have motivated me to speak on behalf of the many African Americans he sometimes forgot about. I would have enjoyed dressing up in the beautiful gowns worn by some of the world's most breathtaking women like Billie Holiday & Josephine Baker. I would wear these beautiful gowns to the Savoy Club and dance the night away, grooving to the sultry sounds of Duke Ellington and Count Basie. If I lived in Harlem during the 1920s, I would probably spend lots of time on Striver's Row getting the attention of those wealthy residents, motivating them to use their wealth and power in a positive way (Personal document, April 24, 2006).

Her reading of this piece succeeded in engaging students and developing their writing (and thinking). In addition to modeling the practice of sharing writing and soliciting feedback from others, it introduced Andrea's interests and politics to students. This provided a concrete example of how, in every piece of writing that people craft, they are sharing a part of themselves.

Overall, the Harlem Renaissance unit embedded the reading and writing skills required by the 5th-grade district curriculum. It also provided students with a sense of their history, engaged them in a literary and artistic tradition, and connected to their current lives. This unit significantly extended the time typically allotted to this content from a week or less to a month. Andrea selected this particular research unit because of her commitment to exposing students to the period's great writers, historians, artists, scientists, and mathematicians, as well as the historical struggles. She had the flexibility to make this decision because of her instructional autonomy and because she embedded literacy skills that were a part of the district standards, thereby creating a new means to mandated goals. As noted in Chapter 2, Andrea had gained an appreciation for the importance of teaching a more inclusive history in high school from a student colleague who angrily resisted what he saw as an exclusionary Eurocentric version of America's founding fathers.

From that moment forward she had realized the importance of restoring the experiences and contributions of African Americans to U.S. history and making connections to the identities of her students.

Andrea was able to take the content skills and standards of the district literacy and social studies curriculum and make the content both academically accessible and relevant to the lives and cultural histories of her students. She intended to draw connections between Black history and her students' contemporary lives with an approach that developed not only their academic skills but also a positive sense of self, particularly related to their racial identities. Andrea's pedagogical approach hooked students into learning and communicated the importance of applying themselves in the moment and in the future. She did not view increased student engagement simply as a goal to improve students' test scores but attempted to lay out a blueprint for how to be participants in their own lives and how to engage with the larger society. This project—like most of what Andrea did in the classroom—facilitated the development of thinking critically about the world, developing a voice, and maintaining a personal style.

BALANCING TESTING PRESSURE WITH INTELLECTUAL ENGAGEMENT

Although the primary content areas for instruction were mathematics for Ellen and literacy for Andrea, both teachers shared an interest in aiding students in developing knowledge beyond that of a narrowly defined subject. As discussed in the previous chapter, Ellen held an ideal of creating social justice mathematicians; educating for social justice was also a goal of Andrea's, and it acted as a guiding force in her curricular decisions. Ayer's (1998) description of teaching for social justice highlights the importance of understanding students' backgrounds, interests, and histories. He presents this philosophical approach as one that "demands a dialectical stance: one eye firmly fixed on the students—Who are they? What are their hopes, dreams, and aspirations? Their passions and commitments? What skills, abilities and capacities does each one bring to the classroom?—and the other eye looking unblinkingly at the concentric circles of context—historical flow, cultural surround, economic reality" (p. xvii).

Andrea aimed to develop critical readers and writers who reflect (and act) on the world (personal communication, February 8, 2006). She believed that literacy facilitates this goal because writing is always partially about the writer. Given this stance, she was able to strengthen reading, writing, and analysis skills at the same time that students were considering who they are in the world, who they wanted to become, and what a better world might look like. Ellen and Andrea were personally motivated to take into account the backgrounds of their students and use this knowledge to inform their instructional practice. They both recognized that the decks are often stacked against individuals solely on the basis of social identities, such as race and class. The teachers eschewed deficit perspectives that framed learners and their families as uncommitted to schooling or that rationalized challenges students may encounter in school as a lack of requisite knowledge, capacities, or skills that it is too late to develop.

The teaching practices of both teachers were predicated on the belief that students were capable and had a great deal to offer to the community of learners they cultivated. Their teaching stances were based on respecting students, believing in their ability to accomplish challenging work, and building on student interests. The teachers believed that if students were well prepared, and if there were facilitated spaces to discuss structural barriers and make the playing field more equal, then students would have better educational opportunities—and, later, more competitive professional opportunities.

Despite the fact that when Ellen transitioned from higher education to middle school mathematics, she was interested in developing her students both as mathematicians and as critical participants in society, she struggled to create space to teach the latter capacities, given the number of set standards students were required to master. At first, she was not convinced of the necessity of standardized assessments; later, she came to believe that they were arguably one of the most important factors for students' futures. After teaching for just 1 year at her current school, she understood that the bottom line was to produce high test scores. She felt that if state exams were the primary measure of student learning, one that would affect the quality of her students' future educational experiences, it was important that students were able to demonstrate their mathematics learning in this way. Although grades and tests were not the primary tools she used to gauge students' understanding, she felt extraordinary pressure from district mandates set in place by state and federal policies. While Ellen believed the benchmarks and assessments represented good mathematical content we can see the ways that state and district pressure influenced the instructional practices and decisionmaking of arguably one of the most qualified, confident, and capable instructors in the state.

Although the majority of her students displayed a motivation to learn, given time pressures to cover state math standards, Ellen turned her attention toward preparing them for the assessment exams by deepening their knowledge of mathematics. Though the state guidelines unfortunately did not emphasize teaching students to be critical thinkers, she felt that if she taught the standards, she could teach "good math" (personal communication, May 4, 2006). By this she meant that she could take any textbook, assignment, or exam and identify the key mathematical concepts being targeted. Given the fact that she is a mathematician who has an exceptional understanding of all the skills and content that make up the curriculum, she was able to boil down the year's work to four key topics and develop students' conceptual understanding. For her, the hallmark of student engagement was students struggling through mathematical thoughts.

On the one hand, Ellen saw the math content and curriculum standards as blueprints for instruction, but she used innovative practices and classroom structures to develop students' understanding. On the other hand, Andrea thought of the curriculum as a loose guide, and she employed alternative methods, texts, and units to move students to the expected target. The architects of new reform strategies such as the CCSS hoped to usher in this type of relationship between teachers' approach to instruction and educational standards. An educational brief on the Common Core explicitly states that they are not intended to dictate teaching, they do not represent everything that should comprise the curriculum, and they do not account for interventions that might be necessary for any student but particularly for advanced students, special needs students, or language minority students.

Andrea did not believe that she risked underpreparing students for state-mandated tests by supplementing and modifying the district curriculum. In fact, in her estimation, students would be better prepared, and she believed that teachers must always make adjustments in curriculum to connect with their students' interests and backgrounds. In an early interview, she stated, "I am not just teaching because . . . this is what the book says I need to do. . . . [I find] out ways that I make sure I can get through to them" (personal communication, April 1, 2005).

Andrea was not limited by the district-mandated literacy curriculum because of her view that teachers should take their backgrounds, professional training, and beliefs to forge a path toward externally imposed goals. She sometimes felt that the amount and frequency of assessments, such as benchmark testing and statewide exams, took away from valuable instruction time. To ensure that the established curriculum met the needs of her students, she added texts that aligned with her students' experiences or ones that pushed them to think in different ways. To supplement books and engage in long-term projects connected to students' life experiences, she had to make modifications, and she did so with the confidence that her choices would be more effective because of her professional knowledge and understanding of students' backgrounds and learning needs.

The approaches taken by these two experienced teachers show us that they have similar goals and stances that lead to different philosophies and strategies for teaching and learning. Both teachers demonstrate success in the classroom as measured by their school and district despite the fact that they experience the standardized curriculum as well as the benchmark and year-end testing as barriers to their instructional goals. Their identities and the identities of the students they teach also influence the decisions they make about curriculum. We must account for these factors when we think about improving teaching and learning because they weigh heavily on student engagement in the learning process.

Classroom-Based Strategies for Engagement

Strategies for classroom-based interventions can be organized by what is taught (content) and by how students are introduced to the content (structures). The previous examples focus on particular curricular units in a mathematics classroom and a humanities classroom. While a focus on curriculum and structure can occur simultaneously, these cases indicate that, often, one instructional mechanism is emphasized over the other. Perhaps as a result of the content area of instruction or how Andrea and Ellen viewed teaching in urban schools, they relied on different mechanisms for engaging learners. Andrea focused on the content of the literacy curriculum, and Ellen more consistently used classroom structures to connect her adolescent learners to mathematics instruction. (The History Data Analysis Project was one major exception.) Ellen felt that she sometimes struggled to reach certain students, but even when it was hard to establish a relationship of mutual trust, she found success using collaborative team structures to engage students and increase their academic growth.

The examples in the next section explore the alternative structures the focal teachers used to accomplish their instructional goals, including the physical layout of the classroom, and how students were organized for their academic work—for example, what academic task structures and social participation structures were used (see Erickson, 1982). Classroom structures and curricula are two key mechanisms to consider when designing interventions aimed at making learning relevant and supporting students' identity-making. These interventions require more than a shift away from the singular focus on coverage of course content in order to demonstrate proficiency on state standardized assessments to deep mathematical understanding. Improving student learning entails building relationships with students through learning about their identities and communities and/or facilitating rather than directing classroom activities in ways that allow students to collaborate with one another and integrate socializing with academic learning.

When we imagine teaching as connected to identity-work, we are cognizant of not only who the students are and their personal stories but also about how teachers' life experiences inform their practice. Teachers can help students think about how history and contemporary events connect to their lives. This teaching and learning exchange can be built on the skills and interests that young people bring to the classroom; as a result, the development of knowledge has a clear purpose—to help people think about the world. When learning is framed in this way, then the classroom community might be engaged in critical analysis of their community and larger world. This approach facilitates questions such as: What in the society needs to change? What role might each individual take in this process for change?

Classroom Structures

Ellen and Andrea recognized the importance of creating flexibility within a larger structure in order to make adjustments in the moment and to create structures within structures that might better meet individual students' needs. Instead of purposefully creating variety in social arrangements for learning, the teachers tended to have an overarching structure; for Ellen, this was small-group work, and for Andrea, a significant amount of instruction was geared toward the entire class, such as encouraging silent and guided reading, individual writing, and class participation and explicitly modeled respectful behavior. Other structures for learning evolved organically or were sporadically created within or in place of typical participation arrangements. Ellen tended to work with students individually or in pairs to tackle challenges they were experiencing, while Andrea felt free to shift the day's agenda as needed, occasionally assigning her students paired or small-group work, as was the case with long-term projects.

Ellen organized her students into permanent teams of four or five (described in greater detail in the next chapter) at the start of the school year with the support of a university professor and a graduate student. She assigned each student to a team of students with whom they would work on a regular basis throughout the course of the year. Groups were configured with at least one student who had demonstrated strong mathematical skills as 6th-graders, and Ellen also placed one of the five students who were not in her class as 6th-graders on each team. Integrating the new students with four 7th-graders with whom she had already spent a year working would allow them the support and modeling from classmates while they acclimated to the style and rigor of this math class.

Students were also assigned to one of five "expert groups": algebra blocks, cognitive tutor, geometry, proportional reasoning, and presentation experts. These groups represented three of the math concepts she expected students to develop a deep knowledge of during their 7th-grade year. Ellen assigned students to their "color group" (purple, red, blue, yellow, or green) based upon their strengths and interests. In certain cases, she identified students who had struggled the previous year and were given extra support so that they would now be comfortable with the topic. The idea was that she would teach the expert and the expert would teach the group. Having taught 21 out of the 25 students, Ellen could take into consideration who worked well together when she formed the groups before the start of the school year (fieldnotes, September 12, 2005).

Ellen found that teaching was much more effective when she worked with small groups, pairs of students, or individually; so, she structured her classroom to allow for these various configurations for learning. Over time, students came to rely on their group members for support as much as, or more than, the teacher. As a result, students not only learned to work together effectively, but they came to know intimately the strengths and mathematical knowledge of each of their team members. One student, Gerald, talked about how the team structure contributed to learning math and learning about his student colleagues.

> I remember math was very easy in 5th grade. And I never had to do any group projects with other people, so I don't really remember much of my classmates, math-wise. In 6th grade it was different 'cause I was in [Dr. Chalmer's] class for the first time and she introduced working in groups, not just groups of one or two, but groups of five people. (personal communication, April 24, 2006)

In assessing the year, Ellen felt that the group structure was a successful tool in motivating students to learn and engaging them in the curriculum. When learning geometry, the members of the expert group in geometry just kept working to figure things out until they were confident in their ability to teach their classmates. They would work on any challenge she handed them, and eventually they were working on high school level geometry using the software Geometer's Sketch Pad.

> The students wouldn't stop. I just kept feeding them more work, and they would work until they mastered it and could teach other people. The experts in the algebra group worked the same way, and so did those students who were cog tutor experts. Students might have said it was learning algebra which kept them engaged but it was the gold bars that were motivating them. (personal communication, June 11, 2006)

The gold bars that Ellen is referring to are the way the individualized adaptive computer program (CogTutor) documented students' competency in an algebraic concept. Students gained confidence and came to share her belief about their ability to learn high-level mathematics concepts. This assumption was an underlying tenant of the decisions she made about classroom structures and the instructional practices she implemented. Ellen intentionally created a classroom where she came to know students' math knowledge as well as their misconceptions in order to increase their levels of understanding. It is her belief that most educators have no idea about the levels of understanding that students are capable of, and therefore teachers do not push students to the levels of understanding that they are capable of achieving. As a result, there is no true sense of students' limits (personal communication, February 2, 2006).

In Andrea's classroom, her chosen type of facilitated discussion created a place where students could engage with text, share their writing, and think critically about new topics to which they were introduced. Schultz (2003) presented a case of a teacher who similarly used classroom discussions "to simultaneously teach the whole group and listen to the individuals within the group. Their purposeful structure gave her a way to accomplish these goals" (p. 49).

Andrea felt that the groundwork on which students build new knowledge ought to be carefully laid. To accomplish her goal of helping students mature in their abilities to constructively criticize both themselves and their peers, she focused on creating a structure with a certain degree of flexibility. When asked what she intentionally put in place to accomplish her instructional goals, she offered the following:

> I think creating that structure within a context that they're familiar with, not trying to really force my beliefs and my way of doing things as an adult, [or] as a teacher. . . . [I take into account] what they have to offer and creating that space but still giving them that flexibility to think and make decisions while also providing them with that structure. (personal communication, May 23, 2006)

Establishing classroom norms, demonstrating engaged learning, and instructing through explicit teacher modeling could be read as practices that place the locus of control in the hands of the instructor, but they also maintain safety and encourage student participation, thus placing the onus of sharing on the student. Andrea continually referenced more general structures of participation, ones that leave space for students' voices and interests. She urged students to look at the speaker who was sharing his or her writing. If students were not ready to share, she guided them in a verbal discussion of their ideas and their intent for the assignment (fieldnotes, September 8, 2005). Also, it was not unusual for Andrea to give students directions about how to sit, where to focus their attention, and what tone they should take with their classmates. Yet attention to the structures and routines of discussion presented the opportunity for students to take ownership of their ideas while growing from perspectives shared by their classmates.

In classroom discussions, Andrea required students to attempt an answer when she called on them, even when they might not have taken advantage of the time to formulate a response during a home assignment or the allotted class period. In fact, this practice, accompanied by close attention to students' behaviors and interactions, is required to maintain a secure space in which students are willing to take risks and reveal their thoughts and feelings. This intent was purposeful and something she shared with students from the very start of the school year. Andrea said:

> I have to compliment the people who are keeping up with the 5th-grade pace. We talked about the fact that we have a lot to learn this year. Some things that belong to you are OK to share with other people. It is OK to feel safe enough to share. (fieldnotes, September 20, 2005)

WORKING WITH AND AROUND MANDATED CURRICULUM

Unlike Andrea and Ellen, some teachers find it difficult to question new national-, state-, and district-level mandates because they are framed as an imperative and the best way to present students with challenging, grade-level material. While recent reforms may be written to allow for teachers to attend to individual learners, the pressure and continued focus on a narrow definition of accountability means that the fact that students need varied types of support, including a curriculum that is clearly tied to their experiences and a content that builds on the knowledge they bring to the classroom, is overlooked.

Ellen is confident that the state math standards and district curriculum are the appropriate materials to help students develop a deep knowledge of math and that these learning goals allow her to push each student to his or her individual capacity. Her mathematical expertise helps her reduce the plethora of units and topics to a handful of key concepts, and her approach to engaging students in this curriculum is unique. As a result of the academic task structures and participatory organization she established in her classroom, the level of math discourse, independent learning, and construction of knowledge was quite advanced for middle school students.

When her class is at its best, Ellen might turn to another adult in the room and ask, in a characteristically joking manner, "Well, should we just go out for coffee and meet them at the end of the period?" While this comment captures the fun and sarcasm that is very much a part of her identity in the classroom, it also reflects her belief in students' ability to learn what they need to know from her so well that they are able to work with their peers to achieve mastery of the essential concepts. However, in full recognition that students need adult support and supervision, much of the time she enlisted college and graduate students and put the student teacher and mentor to work so that on some days, 4 or 5 adults were available to the 25 students in her class. This is a rare opportunity in an urban classroom, one that is possible only because of her school's university partnership. The additional adult support is also a result of the teachers' networking abilities and resourcefulness.

Engagement and Identity Work

Ellen and Andrea are committed to creating an exception to the norm in terms of students' academic growth and social experience. Both teachers assume in their students what Ayers (1998) terms a "great capacity" (p. xxv). As a result of differing racial/ethnic and financial backgrounds and the neighborhoods from which students hail, they recognize that the pupils they teach might not be provided the best educational opportunities and may face contexts that do not fully support them as learners or even entirely respect them as human beings. Their recognition of structural barriers that often limit urban public school students' life options fuels their instructional decisions, focused on rigor, relevance, and relationships. The focal teachers are explicit about what mathematicians and readers/writers must know and be able to do, and they help students develop the conceptual knowledge, strategies, and confidence to tackle grade-level—or advanced—material.

Ellen turns her attention toward developing strong students who will know, but not necessarily like, mathematics and who will be able to pass the state assessments. However, often her students do grow to like—even love—math because of her enthusiasm and ability to develop simultaneously their capacities and their confidence about the mathematics they know and the concepts and skills they can successfully demonstrate. One of her stated goals is for students to "know enough mathematics so they can get through high school whether they have a good teacher or not. And I want them to leave thinking that they will take calculus" (personal communication, October 27, 2005). Although she is less certain about how important it is that the math be connected to students' day-to-day experiences, she is unwavering about the importance of the social exchange in which learning must take place. The structures for participation often situate Ellen on the periphery of her classroom, though the significance of her role is not diminished. When she steps to the center of the teaching stage, she gains her students' complete attention. Her mechanism for engaging students in math learning is most often the participation structure with small groups, student experts, and technology as key features of the process.

While the content area and grade levels that Ellen and Andrea taught likely influenced the approach they took in actualizing their teaching goals, their understanding of student identities also informed their practice. Ellen felt that the math curriculum did not allow her much space to develop knowledge about individual students outside of the classroom. This was coupled with a belief that those matters were not really her concern, and lacking knowledge about certain students' experiences, she therefore found it difficult to make personal connections. In describing her relationship with her students, she noted, "I don't care if they like me. The bottom line is about the learning. The language arts teacher has a great relationship with students. She works really hard and she is a great teacher. They will come to her with more of their personal stuff, and they have a real connection" (personal communication, July 12, 2005). While her position here suggests that a strong personal relationship was secondary to learning, her high expectations, masterful teaching, and respect for students in most cases forged deep relationships with students marked by trust. The rigidness of the math curriculum and pacing schedule yielded less space for identity-work as a central feature of the curriculum, but Ellen used innovative structures and a challenging curriculum to motivate and engage her students.

Andrea saw her role as a teacher as one of preparing her predominately Black and low-income students to become competent readers and writers and gain a sophisticated understanding of their world. Therefore, teaching for understanding included more than a conceptual consideration of content knowledge. What it involved, in Andrea's own words, was having students

> understand the ways of the world. . . . With their reading and with understanding enough to write and articulate, they'll be able to make better choices in life. . . . Because when I look back on my life, everything's happened because I've made certain choices, and [they weren't] always the easiest choice to make. (personal communication, February 8, 2006)

By understanding her students' backgrounds and experiences, Andrea assumes a greater responsibility for changing the course of their lives and becomes more invested in helping youth become agents of change. The commonalities in her and their racial, class, and family background heighten her belief about the importance of teachers instructing by example and sharing who they are in order to engage students and help them find the relationship between their schooling and their day-to-day experiences.

In thinking about students' identities, Andrea recognizes that the students she teaches are different from the youth of past generations.

> They don't have the discipline that we had. So I have to, like, [keep] that in mind. But I know that they have a lot to offer as far as, like, experiences and being very articulate . . . and are already liberated enough to express themselves. So they're going to express themselves. And just thinking about how you create a healthy venue for them to do that . . . and how to let them incorporate writing and reading into their way of thinking. I just know that they aren't the same kids of yesterday. (personal communication, May 23, 2006)

Harnessing Students' Interests and Commitments

Many educators read the behaviors and interests of urban students as incompatible with a traditional model of "school," and they conclude that students are disinterested in academic learning (Carter, 2005; Perry, Steele, & Hilliard, 2003). Andrea did not assume this, but she did see a need to shift instructional practices. The mindset of contemporary youth increases the importance of creating more space in classrooms to both build on and expand students' dispositions. Given that students want to express themselves, they look for every opportunity to talk about their interests and are generally curious and critical of the world around them; Andrea simply identifies a way to structure her curriculum to allow students to discuss and read and write about issues that capture their minds.

As was the case with Ellen, Andrea does this with a larger goal in mind, that of enabling better future educational opportunities for her students that can lead to an increased number of choices in educational, professional, and other life opportunities. In addition to this, Ellen and Andrea hoped that their students not only envisioned but also worked toward a more equitable society.

These instructional strategies point to the importance of teachers gaining autonomy that allows them to make the best decisions for particular students. Sizer (1984) argued that effective schools are those in which teaching decisions are made by the adult closest to the learner, yet our current policies that dictate instruction are made by individuals who are not only far away from the learner but also distant from the schools and communities where such polices have the greatest impact.

Ellen and Andrea used the autonomy they have earned within their school communities to make professional decisions such as adapting curriculum and integrating project-based work that connects students to their history and community. These curricular decisions responded to learner identities; the teachers' knowledge of students' particular needs and interests informed the modifications and additions, while classroom structures allowed students to take ownership of their learning and construct knowledge jointly with peers. They also encouraged students' unique voices and signaled to students that their ideas mattered in the learning process. This stance was predicated on an assumption that students are knowledgeable and capable; it is a stance that values who the learner is and how his or her experiences in the world shape the educational process. This has to be considered in our policy decisions because successful schools are often designed with these principles in mind, but schools that serve children with the greatest amount of need are hampered by reform strategies that decrease students' and teachers' voices while narrowing definitions of curriculum, assessment, and learning.

CHAPTER 4

Classroom Discourse and Identity Work

To some extent, Ellen and Andrea both negotiated between macro- and microanalyses of race, class, and gender oppression though discriminating between these two discourses and understanding the connection between them was a difficult, if not impossible, subtlety for their students to trace. Uncovering how students understood and took up or rejected this discourse can shed light on how best to prepare teachers for classrooms and how to support inservice practitioners in having complex and difficult conversations. What are the cultural models youth apply to make meaning of messages from both teachers and peers about social inequity? To understand this, I examine student and teacher identities through interactions and the particular discourse in use. *Discourse* refers to the social language that is employed to enact certain identities or roles (Gee, 2005). I focus on the discourse around social (in)equity and conceptions of race and ethnicity as it intersects with gender and class identities because of classroom teachers' articulated goals of creating change in the society through teaching. Discourse analysis guided my interpretations of the classroom exchanges, particularly my interpretation of how teachers' and students' schemas interacted and why teacher' intentions were sometimes misunderstood by students because of the different cultural schemas that they carried with them (Gee, 2005). I interpreted student explanations of their experience against the instructional goals that Ellen and Andrea articulated and classroom discourse that developed in each context.

Ellen adopted a stance of combating institutional racism and applied this perspective to her reflection on students' behaviors and actions. This led to a tendency to call out transgressions and was motivated by her belief that a person's uneasiness was to be expected. She felt that if one was forced to reflect upon the way society instills prejudices in everyone, her actions could increase the possibility of change. Rather than separating oppressive structures and institutional policies from individual actions, she identified the complicit participation of administrators, teacher colleagues, and, on occasion, her students in such arrangements in order to raise consciousness about one's thoughts and actions. An example of this was when she challenged her principal and a member of her middle school team about their commitment to maintaining the tracking policy, which she perceived as racist.

Andrea talked about how individuals' choices and responsibilities shape one's condition in conjunction with how social inequity limits opportunities and outcomes for members of minority communities. Students' perspectives help to deconstruct classroom discourse in relation to the sociohistorical context in which teachers teach, paying particular attention to the identities of the individual actors engaged in the dialogue.

A CLASSROOM VIGNETTE

It is the end of February and Dr. Ellen Clay switches gears from a discussion of an upcoming curricular project to a review of students' work on practice tests. The task for the day involves working on an assessment, one that is more difficult than the test students have just completed. Dr. Clay talks openly with students about the progress of different individuals and groups relative to the practice assessments. Addressing an Ethiopian male student, she says, "Here's what you messed up on." Speaking to members of another group whose test scores were the lowest, she teases, "I feel like I have a name for the green group." To this, Randy chimes in and says, "F." Dr. Clay's agreement was signaled by her sarcastic tone, "Yeah, I wonder where I got that name!" Talking about a problem in particular that most students seemed to miss, she notes that both Kieran and Sarah have the question correct. She jokingly identifies the White male and White female students as her "White group" because they have both marked the problem correctly. As it turns out, they have two separate answers and they race to determine who has the correct one. Before she moves on to review the next problem, she says, "In Dr. Clay's class, we do it Dr. Clay's way or she slaps us on the hand." To this, Randy says to no one in particular "and he's bringing an AK47 to kill. . . ." (fieldnotes, February 24, 2006)

By discussing this vignette with Ellen and five of her students who participated in the exchange, I was able to compare the teacher's goals with the students' interpretation of what the teacher was up to. The identification of the two students, both White, who found the right answer on a math problem as her "White group" (as opposed to the actual permanent groups that were identified by color—blue, green, red, yellow, purple) was viewed by students in a number of different ways. The teacher, in revisiting the event, said, "God knows why I referred to those kids as the 'White group' that day. I don't know if we had talked about race or not" (personal communication, May 4, 2006). This remark had occurred in the first ten minutes of class and did not follow a conversation related to race, at least during the math period.

Farah, a Muslim student from Bangladesh, remarked "I don't know if they [other students] thought it was . . . mean or something but I just thought of it as sarcasm" (personal communication, April 6, 2006). Ayo, who identifies as Ghanian and Black American and who had not really thought much of the remark in the moment, said, "I didn't even think—when you first say that like White group, it might sound a little racist but then it is like [the students] must be knowing some White people got it right" (personal communication, May 11, 2006). Ayo's reflections in particular led to a conversation about race, racism, and privilege. She understood this remark and others she had heard in the classroom to be biased. When I asked what she believed the teacher meant by the comment, she replied, "Sometimes she says things that are racist" (personal communication, April 20, 2006). This expression surprised me particularly because Ayo believed she could be herself in the classroom as long as it comported with her role as a student. She characterized her relationship between her and Ellen as most like a friend. She describes her teacher as unlike most teachers, funny but serious about teaching math with an uncanny ability to describe mathematical concepts (personal communication, April 20, 2006).

Later, when Ayo shared a different example of what she perceived to be a negative race-based comment, I shared how I understood Ellen's message based upon my conversations with the teacher—including a discussion about the event Ayo described, which took place just the day before our interview. Ellen talked to me about an incident involving three students in her 8th-grade class: a Black male who was in need of academic support, a White male, and a White female. After suggesting that the White students were responding to their classmates in a racist manner because they would not help him with the assigned group task, she took an opportunity to have a one-on-one discussion with the White male student. In this conversation, she attempted to expose him to the structural realities of race in order to encourage him to support his classmates. Ellen reported that "at the end of the conversation I said, 'so tell me . . .' I was kind of joking, I shook his hand and said, 'so welcome to Race 101 with Dr. Clay.' He said, 'When's our next class?' So he was excited and I did not follow up on that" (personal communication, June 19, 2006). For Ellen, this represented a rare moment when she could raise issues related to race and racism with students and explore social inequity and how it related to math learning. She believed it was a positive encounter that would force students to consider their racial identities in ways that could build a stronger collective identity among students.

After offering my interpretation of the event based upon this conversation with Ellen (and others), I probed to understand from Ayo the types of remarks she would categorize as racist. Ayo identified the same event that is described above between Ellen and a White male, in her 8th-grade math classroom. Ayo's description of this incident, which was the perspective of another 8th-grade boy, varied significantly from what Ellen had shared in our conversation. Ayo reported that she had a friend from another class (a Black male) whom Ellen pulled into a conversation about getting support from his peers. Ellen later had a conversation with him where she explained that she had certain privileges that she was afforded just because she was White, but that he, an 8th-grade African American boy, would be viewed in a certain way and that people would not provide him with the same kind of access or support she received because he's Black (personal communication, April 20, 2006). In Ayo's retelling of this interaction, she understood a very different message conveyed to her friend by the teacher. Her understanding of the exchange was based upon a conversation with her friend, and she reported the following: "Dr. Clay pulled him to the side and after everybody left to go down to lunch, he came down and told us that Dr. Clay was like, she got to a higher place because she's White, and he's just Black and that's why he's stupid or whatever" (personal communication, April 20, 2006).

An interaction experienced by Ellen as an opportunity to push students to examine the social and institutional forces that cause inequity was read by Ayo as an example of her teacher's racism. Ayo believed her teacher was suggesting that her success was due to her race and that her Black male friend was not smart and would not be successful because of his race. Ayo and her friend believed that their teacher viewed the boy as stupid and in need of more support. This example demonstrates that it is not simply students' or teachers' identities that inform how social–cultural–economic issues are communicated and understood but the context in which such complex topics are raised. The cultural model that Ayo brings is connected to her status as a Black person in America who is often viewed by White people as less capable. Rather than notice that Ellen is trying to uncover the way that White people are unjustly privileged in society and Black people are often not given the opportunities or supports to be successful, the meaning she makes is that Ellen believes Black people to be stupid and White people more worthy.

Student responses to the vignette in Ellen's room prompted me to wonder what conditions would be necessary for White middle-class teachers to talk productively about race with a diverse group of students. When attempts were made by Ellen to address hierarchical structures related to race in the American context, at least one student understood her remarks as racist. Ayo's perception of these events raises the possibility that racial and ethnic identities make it complicated for students to differentiate between moments when teachers are trying to talk about race openly, when they are trying to create access for and with people of color when they have historically been denied entry, or when they are engaged in practices or discourses that might perpetuate stereotypes. This is one example of how students understood teacher practice through their individual identities, particularly related to their race/ethnicity, gender, ability, and socioeconomic status.

SOCIAL ISSUES AND THE CURRICULUM

There were distinctly different discourses about difference in the two classrooms that informed Ellen's and Andrea's approaches to instruction. At least three significant factors related to how social issues were taken up and discussed in class that informed curricular decisions, including the facility with which topics could be integrated into the curriculum, the content area of instruction and the prescribed curriculum, and teachers' understanding of the teaching role as instructor of content versus teacher–mentor. A notable feature of classroom practice, and in particular how social issues were engaged, is linked to differences between Andrea's and Ellen's classrooms. In Andrea's classroom there was a formal integration of history, social movements, personal experience, and discussions about how social identities inform one's position in contemporary society into the language arts curriculum. In contrast, Ellen felt she had to create spaces outside the bounds of the formal curriculum to address students' experiences and social issues.

Ellen believed that students reacted negatively or were not interested when she raised racial issues. I paid particular attention to this assertion in my observations so that I might understand students' reactions and sentiments. I began to consider if and why students wanted to avoid talking about difference. Was this related to Ellen's race, or to the fact that her students came from a diversity of racial and ethnic backgrounds, or perhaps to the context in which the issues were raised? From my observations I learned that when race was interjected into the classroom discourse it was most often a tangential topic of conversation or sidebar statements or questions. Rarely was race put directly on the table for an academic investigation or discussion.

A number of times racial issues were presented as a joke such as the time when a teacher was visiting during math class. Ellen started off the period with a math game. Students called out answers to the questions she posed and Randy was in the thick of the competition. He offered a wrong answer and, at the same time, the visitor, a young White woman, offered the correct solution. Presumably to motivate Randy, and to have a little fun, Ellen chided, "What? Are you going to let a White lady beat you?" (fieldnotes, February 27, 2006). This was a brief moment, where the playful barb at Randy called upon his demonstration of competence over another racial group in the math game. While there was no demonstrative reaction by Randy or any other student to this remark, I offer it to show how discourses of race were occasionally interjected into the classroom on the fly and unconnected to instructional content.

A more deliberate context to investigate social identities arose when students were given the opportunity to frame their own research questions connected to the Historical Data Analysis Project, described in Chapter 3. This unit was conducted in May, less than 2 months before the end of the school year, and it provides a counter-example to a playful or peripheral insertion of race and inequity. The data unit was embedded in a local historical project where the math curriculum was focused on connecting to students' lives as residents of a particular community. Students interacted with primary source documents (census data) from the early 20th century and crafted research questions along with their group members based upon interesting patterns in the data. In this unit students were able to look at race, class, and gender within their project of study and offer a historical analysis of the topic, given the primary source data reviewed. The questions were authentic interests they held, and although they were not all answerable (given the data set) students became more informed about education, jobs, and the demographics of their community during the early 1900s. In the data project investigations students were comfortable with discourse around race, class, and gender. They did not shy away from the topics when embedded in the math curriculum; in fact, they initiated inquiry into a variety of social issues.

When issues of race and equity were deliberately structured and integrated with curriculum inquiry, students tended to be open to engaging, although finding the space for this work could be a challenge in a math classroom. There were also times when the topics hit too close to home, and students resisted participating in classroom writing or discussing these issues. This was the case in Andrea's 5th-grade literacy classroom when she asked students to read a short story by Toni Cade Bambara (2004) entitled *Geraldine Moore the Poet*. The text is about a young girl who is expected to attend school, engage in classroom activities, and complete her homework while her mom is sick and away from home. Geraldine is "looked after" by neighbors, an elder sister, or herself—as a result she often goes without meals. The day that she returns from lunch, after watching men carry her family's furniture to the front lawn (they are being evicted) she tells her teacher that she has not composed a poem for homework because "nothing lovely has been happening in my life" (Bambara, 2004). After reading Bambara's story, the class was asked to make text-to-self connection. The students had a good deal of practice with this strategy, and most had a great deal of trust in their teacher. There were many connections to be drawn between the text and students' lives, but they refused to engage with this assignment. Talking about their experience with hunger, parental absence, eviction, or other life challenges that might affect their participation in school was not safe territory, at least not to share with their peers. Students might have drawn a connection to the text that did not make them vulnerable, or situate them as poor, but very few could imagine that possibility, so they claimed that nothing in the text applied to their lives.

Andrea tended to talk about race, gender, and inequity regularly, but more often she talked about individual lives and the possibility of improving oneself and contributing to change in the world, rather than present a structural analysis of race or class dynamics. There were opportunities in the language arts curriculum to investigate historical and social issues connected to people of color, and there were also numerous ways that Andrea was able to integrate such topics into the standard curriculum. This included recognizing the contribution of African Americans through a study of the civil rights movement and the Harlem Renaissance, composing a biography of a famous African American person, and taking a class trip to the Blacks in Wax Museum in Baltimore, Maryland. Informed by her belief that "writing is always about who you are," she used her identity and experiences as a pedagogical tool. Her physical presence offered a model of someone who came from a similar racial group and class background as her students who was able to change the trajectory of her life through education and responsible choices. This success not only provided Andrea more opportunities, it also situated her in a position to make change in the world. Andrea would say that this was because her family made good choices for her and because throughout her life Andrea also made positive decisions and took advantage of opportunities despite the fact that at times she endured tremendous struggle. Andrea's teaching goals emphasized providing the kind of academic background and social development that would lead students to a range of choices in the future. She compelled her students to be conscious of decisions they made, including their use of instructional time. She constantly encouraged students to assess if they were making the best choice at any given moment. This is related to her belief that people of color must take on personal responsibility and pursue the same opportunities as those from the majority culture in the United States. She imagines her life is an example of how individual responsibility and self-improvement can bring about change.

Students seemed to internalize this discourse, and they were willing to take ownership of, or at least place responsibility on, underresourced communities of color to change the social environments they inhabited. During a meeting with four focal students from Andrea's classroom, we revisited the topics of study during the year. I asked students about what they had learned and how they felt about doing research projects, and it sparked a discussion about whether there had been much change in the social conditions of various racial groups. When a student suggested that a lot of improvements occurred between the Harlem Renaissance and the civil rights movement, the class moved to a discussion of what had changed and what issues remained the same in contemporary America. Reggie stated that things were "still not the way they [civil rights activists] wanted it" and he offered the following examples:

> *Reggie:* People not caring for the neighborhood. Destroying, throwing food on the ground. And while they're eating in the car just throw it out. Or people urinate on people's lawns and stuff and don't care what happens. Or other people spray graffiti on other people's properties or school property.

CJW: Okay. So one of the things is taking care of community, and looking out for our neighborhoods, and that's something we'd like to change still. What about in terms of relationships or in terms of opportunities for people?

Anthony: I don't really think people [are] like talking. I hear a lot of things on the streets—people getting—Black and White people getting shot. Or little kids getting shot because two others were shooting and she got shot, and . . . (fieldnotes, June 16, 2006)

Sandra, a member of the focus group, indicated that she was not clear about what the group was discussing so Cherise summarized our conversation in the following way: "We're talking about how we think the world has changed and what we like about it and what we don't like about it. . . . What I don't like about it is that [there is] too much Black-on-Black crime" (fieldnotes, June 16, 2006).

This exchange demonstrated that 5th-graders have a sense of social issues and were likely to apply an analytic lens that had been introduced to them by their teacher. The influence of Andrea's cultural frame was threaded through the discussion as it moved from questions of individual responsibility, to social inequity, to community action. Students identified genuine problems including neighborhood decline, the use of tobacco and alcohol, community violence, and the increase in shootings, as well as other instances of Black-on-Black crime. The issues they identified might not be ones that have directly affected their families, but they were certainly related to conditions to which students lived in close proximity. The focal students declared the need for change, and they saw themselves as participants in such a project. Reflecting upon their literacy curricular units was the starting point for their analysis, and I suspect that the months of historical discussion connected to contemporary problems informed their thinking. As Reggie suggested, the class research project, biographies of famous African American people helped them "experience and learn more about their culture" (fieldnotes, June 16, 2006). Exposure to Black culture was an explicit goal of their teacher, and it was also an activity that students identified as important by the end of the year.

Andrea often supplemented the district curriculum with texts and projects that would speak to students' interests and identities, allowing them to make sense of the material while gaining a better sense of themselves. Discussion about difference and inequity were almost always grounded in history or literature (the content areas of instruction). Students were open to these conversations because they understood them as a central feature of their course of study. The interrogation of social inequity was normalized and students' personal development was attended to as a transparent goal of learning, both of which grounded the classroom discourse. There was an explicit attention to sociohistorical issues and a discourse developed that functioned in two ways: it gave students a way to articulate Andrea's cultural models, and it provided language for them to evaluate the models for themselves and provide critiques.

> I think I start from where I am and my different experiences . . . in preparing them for the future, and think about what's relevant and what's not relevant and that time factor. So I guess strategically thinking about sometimes creating those experiences for them and how deep should I go. I know some of my colleagues, some of them are teaching at the high school level, they really go deep and dive right in and talk about this whole thing, about differences and they're maybe more explicit with those type of experiences. But I think about those types of things and social justice. I think I'm more implicit. (personal communication, July 26, 2006)

The classroom-level discourse on race, class, and gender inequity in the two classrooms informed students' perceptions and their willingness to examine such topics. Andrea attempted to expose students to inequity at the micro- and macrolevels while providing them with tools to critically engage these issues. She was careful not to overwhelm her 5th-graders or give them the impression that social hierarchies are immutable. This stance requires a careful balance between examinations of structural versus individual remedies toward progress. Her emphasis on the potential for the individual to make change could be understood as a tool of empowerment or as an over-deterministic responsibility placed upon the individual to change his or her circumstances.

Ellen is more squarely focused on macrolevel issues—namely, segregation, poor educational opportunities for less resourced communities, and the unearned privileges afforded to White people. Ellen remained committed to identifying school policies and practices that reinforced institutional inequity even though this stance might lead to her being ostracized by colleagues. She pointed to decisions or practices that she perceived as inequitable, sometimes racist, with fellow teachers or students. Leveling such a charge in contemporary American society is hard-hitting, but, in an effort to confront injustice, she willingly called issues as she saw them. In this way she was also concerned with microlevel forces, looking to identify and confront discrimination not only in structures and policies but also in individual interactions.

SOCIAL GROUPS, SOCIAL IDENTITIES

While teachers have a central role in framing classroom discourse, the youth who inhabit the space of the classroom also shape the language-in-use. The norms and facilitative role that teachers assume can positively influence student-to-student exchanges, although youth culture will often take on a life of its own. In an effort to understand student experiences and consider their role in constructing the classroom culture, I met with five students in each classroom individually and as a group. In conversations with the students, I inquired about how social relationships affected the way peers viewed each other. I also asked about how differences were marked in students' immediate world, having explored teachers' views on teaching across difference.

Two girls, Ayo and Zora, both of whom have an African parent but identify as African American, attempted to say that they were sometimes judged based upon how they looked and that assumptions were made about their background. Ayo argued, "People like to judge people based on what they look like. They judge them by the cover; they don't even take a second to read the book or something." She began to share an example of this from another school she attended, but became silent and decided that she did not have an example, or at least one that she was willing to share in this multiracial group that included four of her classmates. Zora offered, "People don't accept who you are sometimes, like somebody who might be jealous or something, they'll be like uh she's snobby or she's conceited or something like that but they probably don't know your background or where you come from or something like that" (fieldnotes, June 16, 2006). A White male student countered with the following comment:

> To be quite honest, I don't really think people do relate about their ethnicities, because I really never had any real . . . or heard of any real problems about . . . People talk more like kids to kids, and not South to West [neighborhoods of the city] or Bangladesh to Pakistan. That's never happened . . . although people do take pride in where they're from. (fieldnotes, June 16, 2006)

The same boy, Gerald, who identifies as a Quaker, suggested moments later that all the Muslim students "hang out" because they feel more comfortable together. When challenged by Farah, a Muslim girl in the group, he apologized immediately, but he still insisted that people would be more comfortable with individuals who were from a background similar to theirs.

> Well, if you're from the same neighborhood, you have . . . your parents have similar jobs; you both grow up in basically the same way, same school and everything. When you grow up, you're gonna feel very, you're gonna feel way more comfortable to them, whereas as compared to some hippie from California who grew up with his mother being a CEO for something. Because that's really nothing like you and how you grew up. (fieldnotes, June 16, 2006)

The examples students shared about how social groups are organized related to students' interests and personalities. Some students also believed that students' backgrounds (social status, religion, phenotypic features) had a great deal to do with who socialized with whom and how these groups were viewed. In the same conversation we discussed whether students' identities or the groups with which they were associated affected their interactions with teachers. As we have seen, Randy articulated a clear sense of how he was viewed by students and teachers, but some might argue that his outward behavior only served to reinforce their assumptions. His behavior, might be read as a "tough front"(Dance, 2002), a performance of hypermasculinity employed as a protective coping mechanism. It is possible that Randy is intentionally performing a stereotype he perceives others hold of him. Another interpretation is that he is resisting the roles that are afforded to him and still managing to perform successfully despite the constraints of the identity he is ascribed by his peers (and some of his teachers). During one focus group meeting, the students' conversation about how peer groups and other collective identities influenced teachers' views of students quickly shifted from the hypothetical to the real and landed Randy on the hot seat.

> *CJW:* Does the group you hang out with affect your relationships . . .
> *Randy:* It affects your relationships with cops.
> *Gerald:* If you do drugs!
> *Randy:* If you are from a [neighborhood] where the cops try to pick on people and try to get people in trouble.
> *Zora [to Randy]:* So the cops are racist?
>
> *Randy nods his head to say yes*
>
> *Gerald:* Come on, this isn't the 50s! (fieldnotes, June 16, 2006)

While this exchange represented how interactions might occur between the youth and authority figures outside of the classroom context, it was significant because it revealed how differently students viewed social contexts, as well as how the nature of individual interactions and experiences differed. Students were not only questioning Randy's meaning, but they were also challenging his assertion that racism still affects relationships between police officers and community members. They were calling Randy to task about his use of marijuana, and I am sure they believed they were exposing this fact to me. In our earlier individual interview, Randy admitted to using "weed" in the past, and he shared with me the serious consequences he endured at home for this decision. This group of students could not conceive that two realities might coexist; the idea that Randy was occasionally involved in dubious activities in his neighborhood and that he had been mistreated and harassed by police without provocation remained an unconsidered possibility.

Randy's experience and perspective were delegitimized by his peers simply by their response to his statements. The way he was positioned by his classmates prohibited the opportunity to learn from Randy if there were, in fact, incidents he had endured that would provide evidence of the discriminatory ways that cops operate in urban contexts (Swanson, Spencer, Dell'Angelo, Harpalani, & Spencer, 2002). In this instance, it was a White boy and an African American girl who disputed Randy's claims and moved the focus of discussion away from racial profiling and harassment to Randy's inappropriate behavior. Randy did not abandon his attempt to be heard when the topic shifted to a conversation about how teachers love students who are in a "smart [peer] group." He added that his group of friends disliked one of the middle school teachers to which Gerald quickly retorted that most students shared their sympathies. Randy continued by pointing out that when his friends were not on task she paid attention, but other students who played around went unnoticed by this teacher (fieldnotes, June 16, 2006). Although Randy did not draw an explicit link between the cops' treatment of him and his friends in his neighborhood and teacher's treatment of his peer group, in both cases the groups targeted were male youth of color. Only one of the five students in the group was White, but he was the only Black male and he presented an opinion that was not shared by others. As a result students delegitimized his perspective and constrained his social position. In doing so, they were communicating that they viewed him as a certain kind of person, the kind of person whose perspectives should not be taken at face value (Foucault, 1995).

In individual student interviews I asked each student who they perceived as smart in their classroom and who their peers viewed as smart. This question was initially motivated by the posting of test scores in Ellen's classroom and an attempt to understand how students made sense of teachers' construction of a successful student. When this question was posed to Quan, a student in Andrea's classroom, he identified two girls as smart in addition to Reggie, and then he added, "the whole class is smart" (personal communication, June 1, 2006). This is notable because Reggie arrived as a struggling student who was slated to be in a self-contained special education classroom. Over the course of the year, his literacy skills developed by leaps and bounds, as did his confidence and test scores. Quan let on that he was including all of his classmates in his response because he feared someone would be angry if they found out he did not identify them as smart.

Ayo responded to this question by saying, "I think everybody's smart in their own ways" (personal communication, June 1, 2006). Her statement stood in contrast to remarks that the other 7th-grade students from Ellen's class offered and pointed to her inclusivity and how she framed intelligence. The 7th-graders shared honest opinions about their classmates in terms of how they were viewed intellectually and personally and the perceptions teachers and students held about them. With the exception of Ayo, the four other focal students named the White and Asian students (Chinese, Bangladeshi), as well as a girl from Egypt, as individuals who were the smartest in their class. Although most students identified the same three or four students, when Farah named four White students as smart, she offered the following qualifications: "Gerald is smart, but sometimes he doesn't act like it. He's hyper. . . . I think Vadim's smart . . . like Vadim he doesn't really show how smart he is . . . he doesn't show his smartness. But when he does do something like Math 24 [a math card game] he's really fast and he was good (personal communication, April 24, 2006). At the last minute, she added a Chinese girl, and then stated that there are a lot of smart students in the class and named three additional students, one of whom was Black (Ethiopian).

Despite Ellen's purposeful challenges to typically held notions of "good students," the children she taught seemed to focus solely on performance as demonstrated through test scores and grades. She identified a broad range of her students as smart, and the variety of student's gender, race/ethnicity, religion, and class background were equally represented. This is an example where her beliefs about the capacity of all students did not translate to students' beliefs about others, perhaps because the larger sociohistorical frames had taken a strong hold in students' minds by this point in their academic career.

HOW CLASSROOM DISCOURSE INFORMS IDENTITIES

When I asked students about classroom incidents, I created a space for them to reflect upon and articulate when and how they felt understood, or perhaps misunderstood, by their peers, teachers, or other adults in the community. An example of this pattern was captured in the exchange previously described when a student's experience related to race and racial discrimination was silenced because of the singular category of person (pot head) his classmates had assigned to him. The classroom discourse and larger social models influenced students' support or lack of support for their peers. Not surprisingly, teachers' interpretations of student identities mediate these processes.

When Ellen attempted to inform students about the realities of institutionalized inequity, her message was often misunderstood and sometimes rejected by her students. As I have previously stated, the content, the demographics of her group, and the fact that such issues were not easily integrated into the math curriculum all played a significant role in how students experienced her message. In Andrea's classroom, due to the fact that there were openings to study historical and contemporary social issues, investigations into how social identities informed peoples' experience were made a central part of her curriculum. Andrea attempted to provide her students with a structural analysis of social inequality at the same time that she emphasized the responsibility and power of the individual to make change. The stance teachers took informed the classroom level discourse about identities and inequality. For example, Andrea's students moved between identifying school district policies based upon race and socioeconomic status that disadvantaged them, on the one hand, and placing responsibility for the deterioration of the Black community on individuals in the community who drank, smoked, littered, and used violence to solve disputes, on the other hand.

The way that social issues are connected to curricular content and classroom events informs the meanings students produced. In addition to the content area and the standard curriculum informing the facility with which teachers could integrate or attend to social issues, how teachers conceptualized their teaching role related to the framing of classroom discourse. Rather than making an argument about the identity of students as learners, I illustrate how teachers' views of students informed their experiences and influenced their engagement in the learning process. Teachers' instructional goals were very clearly tied to their strategies for social improvement as well as to their interest in helping students progress academically (and most often) socially. Understanding students as both learners and individuals in the world is central to the educational process. Ellen and Andrea both had an explicit goal of knowing students' strengths and challenges and understanding their learning style. Ellen thought first of developing mathematicians and then focused on developing relationships with individual students when they were not academically engaged.

Ellen and Andrea were both committed to helping students understand how micro exchanges and macro structures related to race, class, gender, and nationality shaped individual experiences, but it was difficult if not impossible for their students to discriminate between these discourses and to understand the connection between them. A variety of factors contribute to this challenge, such as the experience and developmental age of students, the differences in cultural models between teacher and student, and general misunderstandings that are typical of regular communication. Even given these factors, the recognition that students sometimes misunderstood, took up, and other times rejected the social equity discourse has considerable implications for how teacher preparation programs are designed and the types of professional development opportunities that are made available to educators. If teachers can carefully attend to the conditions in which race, privilege, and inequitable social structures are raised, these conversations will be more successful. In general, the norms and culture of the classroom have to be explicitly established by administrators and teachers in order to safely take on these complex topics. The examples teachers present to students for their consideration need to be clear and purposefully constructed. The curriculum, school policies, and instructional goals should afford the teacher, and the students, opportunities to fully explain the issues at hand as well as the historical background. Space and time must be allotted to debrief what is heard and how people feel about the conversation. Given the reality of a standardized math curriculum and frequent benchmark testing, the time and opportunities to frame and investigate such topics is difficult to locate. As a result, how students experienced the learning environment and teaching goals in some cases was different from what the teacher intended. A series of brief in-the-moment decisions aimed at putting race and racial inequity on the table often did not yield the response or understanding that Ellen was trying to achieve.

The classroom discourse and interactions between students and teachers shaped students' experiences in the classroom and informed how they saw themselves and how others viewed various individuals. Teachers' cultural models shaped the discourse of the classroom, and students made meaning of these discourses by drawing upon their own cultural models. This process highlights how identities are coconstructed through interactions between a teacher and students and also how there are particular cultural experiences that are central to defining how one is understood and how one comes to understand others. If in fact "identities are fashioned from the limited repertoire of understanding ourselves and our lives made available to us in public discourse" (Bettie, 2003, p. 195), then the classroom becomes a critical space for expanding discourse and engaging in identity-work.

CHAPTER 5

Inquiry Into Teaching

In Boston in 1995 an experiment was launched that few districts had ever attempted: The strategy was to place responsibility for a school's success on teachers and school leaders, while also giving them complete autonomy to decide how to achieve their goals. Teachers (and their principals) were granted control over the school's budget, staffing, curriculum, and school calendar. The hope was that this decisionmaking power would spark innovation and create effective practices that would dramatically improve student learning (French, Miles, & Nathan, 2014). In exchange for increased autonomy, teachers were held accountable for their students' progress and for the health and well-being of the institution. This meant that if a school was not living up to the mission or students were not demonstrating academic progress, then that school would be closed.

The resulting Boston Pilot School Network was a local innovation that grew out of the concerns that the Boston Public Schools district (BPS) was losing too many students to newly forming charter schools. BPS granted "charter-like" autonomy to a category of schools that remained under the umbrella of the district. These schools would be designed with considerable input from parents, educators, and district personnel. Since the initial five pilot schools created in 1995, there were 45 autonomous public schools in Boston by 2013, representing six types of schools: pilots, Horace Mann charters, turnaround, innovation, in-district transformation, and receivership schools (For the different description of autonomous school types see French et al., 2014.)

The report by French, Miles, and Nathan (2014) on the success of autonomous schools in Boston pointed out that efforts to improve schools required changes in policies to empower school leaders and teachers with autonomy, accompanied by constructive accountability structures. Together, these elements contributed to improvements in learning and teaching in these schools. According to the report, much of the credit for these measurable improvements should be given to the key decisionmaking authority handed to teachers, who are often best equipped to identify the needs of the students in their charge. When teachers are empowered to make critical decisions about the school and their curriculum, they are inclined to reflect upon their own professional experiences and focus on supports they need to be most effective, while centering their attention on the voices and needs of students. One school leader pointed out that school autonomy allowed teachers "to think about what skills we want to teach, how we want to assess them and what is the most supportive setting in which students can learn" (French et al., 2014, p. 55). School autonomy is a necessary but not sufficient condition for school success. However, it must be paired with accountability because greater autonomy alone will not lead to vastly improved student and teacher outcomes. Boston is one of five large urban districts nationally that has autonomous school models other than charters; Baltimore, Denver, Los Angeles, and New York also have expanded models of in-district autonomous school structures. In each of these urban districts, autonomy is coupled with a strong system of accountability (e.g., portfolio review, annual report card, school quality review). Failure to increase performance within a 3–5-year cycle can lead to removal of a principal, district intervention, replacing the school, or school closure.

This system of accountability may sound similar to the mandates of school closure under NCLB, but they are quite different. One way the accountability system differs from the system outlined under NCLB is in the freedom and flexibility granted to schools, enabling teachers to design individualized educational missions, curriculum, and their own professional development plan. These schools often incorporate the previously described model of embedded professional development, which leads to collaborative teacher work and reflective practice. Another significant divergence is that the district and the state Department of Education instituted structured systems of accountability to document progress and to expose areas of concern, prior to making high-stakes decisions, including those concerning new governance or school closure. When initially implemented in 2000 in Boston, the school quality review outlined five focus areas with established criteria that became the basis of a self-study and then an external review. The areas of focus consist of vision, governance, teaching and learning, professional development, and family/community relationships.

This is one example of an accountability system designed to provide an optimal learning experience for both adults and young people. In this model there is little room for stalled learning, because stakeholders are allowed to build on their experiences and professional knowledge when providing input to improve teaching outcomes, particularly with respect to the identities of the students whom they serve. As a result, these stakeholders often feel an emotional investment toward the institution's success. In the Boston Pilot Schools, academic standards and goals for graduates are set by those who are most knowledgeable, and the process of accountability requires the schools to document, reflect on, and take stock of the goals that they themselves have articulated.

Whether characterized by curriculum, district standards, or the recent Common Core State Standards, effective instruction requires that individual teachers establish goals and devise pedagogies to most effectively present the curriculum to students. This must occur with the background of the teachers in mind as well as the identities, experiences, and needs of the students. While standards are relatively static in nature, they identify a general goal, but not the path to that goal. Curricula should be one tool teachers use to support students as they endeavor to reach an established competency. It is always transformed by the teachers, given their capacities, interests, and goals, as well as by the qualities of the students under their tutelage. In autonomous schools teachers have authority over curriculum and are provided the space to develop deep and meaningful relationships with their students during the course of teaching.

Regrettably, district-based autonomous schools are the exception rather than the rule in the national education landscape. In most traditional urban schools, teachers are under tremendous pressure to improve students' scores on standardized tests or Common Core assessments. The popular strategies for urban school reform focus on metrics, limit teachers' understanding of learning, and often hamper the creation of the best educational contexts to support teaching and learning. Instead, teachers report feeling forced to design instructional plans that are focused on their students' standardized test performances. Because of the pressure to produce adequate standardized test scores, many teachers feel they are given prescriptive models that limit their ability to rely on their expertise and make pedagogical adjustments based on the students they are teaching.

In 2006 I concluded a research project with the following proposition: "until as much attention is paid to supporting teachers to effectively engage students and to helping teachers interrogate practices, with attention to their beliefs and goals, as is paid to the implementation and assessment of a standardized curriculum, improvement in students' learning will be measured if not stalled" (Jones-Walker, 2008). Unfortunately, my point has been proven time and again in the intervening years; indeed, it is one reason that the federal government has initiated a "work-around" the NCLB Act, namely waivers. A network of schools in Boston and four other urban centers stand as exceptions. The question to consider is what made the growing cohort of autonomous schools in Boston effective when so many other urban districts are failing to make progress?

WHAT DOES SCHOOL AUTONOMY AFFORD?

The example of teachers in Boston underscores the importance of teacher autonomy and the strengths of teacher-led networks and planning. Chapter 3 outlined the various ways that teachers use autonomy to create engaging curriculum, to teach with an eye toward social justice, to present intellectually rigorous content, to build deep relationships with learners, to show students that their experience and voice matter, to "work around" mandated curriculum, and to trust that their adaptations will lead to more prepared learners. Having power over key instructional decisions has been shown to be an important factor in teacher motivation and job satisfaction (Ingersoll & Alsalam, 1997). In addition, having autonomy over what happens in the classroom is the greatest single influence on teachers staying in their schools (Ingersoll & Alsalam, 1997; Pearson & Moomaw, 2005). Increased autonomy over curriculum also lowers on-the-job stress (Pearson & Moomaw, 2005). Thus, greater autonomy in general leads to teachers feeling more empowered, whereas constraints on teacher autonomy lead to more tension and anxiety for the educator.

Alignment of Identity and Teaching Goals

The Boston model also worked for another reason: Teachers were allowed to align their identity and their vision of what teaching means with their classroom practice. In this model, teachers worked in grade-level or content-area teams to design and plan what they would teach and to problem-solve around students' conceptual or skills-based challenges. In these small autonomous schools, teachers also worked in advisory teams to address the socioemotional issues faced by students, with whom they met regularly to support them in a generalized way, both as learners and as individuals. In a context designed to ensure that each child was known well by at least one adult in the community beyond a specific content area, intimate relationships developed between the teachers and each learner. Armed with this understanding of students, teachers then were well positioned to make appropriate decisions about curriculum, pedagogical strategies, assessments, and school policies.

Inquiry and Collaboration

Teacher autonomy not only facilitates more informed decisionmaking related to the content and the individual needs of students, it also allows teachers to plan, think, and act. In autonomous schools teacher collaboration and inquiry are often the norm—through this shared work identity-making occurs. Collaboration and inquiry require reflection and problem posing. This approach necessitates that educators develop an understanding of their own strengths and challenges as well as how their previous experiences in the world inform who they are and what they believe. Pedagogical models and accountability structures that are designed with the least prepared or least qualified teacher in mind prefer that educators do not think for themselves or take instructional decisions into their own hands.

    A group of 17 early- to midcareer teachers who were selected to participate in an Urban Teacher Leadership Institute shared what drew them into teaching during one-on-one interviews. The majority of these teacher–leaders, who were convened over several years at two summer institutes and several intervening meetings, expressed a commitment to social justice as a key factor that attracted them to the profession. Many also said that they wanted to develop deep relationships with young people through a teaching–learning partnership (Tamir, 2013). Other studies have identified similar "pulls" into the classroom (Oakes, Franke, Quartz, & Rogers, 2002; Tamir, 2009). If knowing students well and thinking about preparing young people to be agents of change in society are central reasons that attract teachers to teaching, then the conditions and environment in many traditional schools are unsatisfactory for developing and sustaining educators.

Typically, teachers care about students beyond their ability to engage and perform academically. As a result, connecting academic content to events outside of the classroom would be welcomed because it builds connections and relationships at once. Teachers are predisposed to analyze their classroom exchanges and their relationships with colleagues, so it is apparent that we should create the space for this to happen in constructive ways that foster and build on professional capacities. Teachers who join the profession to advance social justice are poised to think about their background and beliefs and how their experiences in the world inform the teaching philosophy and pedagogy they develop. These practices—designing authentic work, building relationships with students, analyzing classroom events, reflecting on teaching with colleagues—are the key elements of identity-work, integral to the process of changing beliefs and improving instructional practices. School autonomy and teacher leadership are critical conditions if the goal is to have decisions about teaching and learning occur closest to the learner. Teachers' perspectives ideally provide a whole picture of the student, which leads to better decisionmaking. Almost without exception, the insights gained from the teacher–student relationship yield richer, more complex data about students than what can be gleaned by their performance on standardized tests. This knowledge, paired with the time and space for reflection and analysis of interactions among fellow practitioners, is likely to yield benefits for teachers, students, and the larger school community.

CRITICAL INCIDENTS AS A TOOL FOR IDENTITY-WORK AND IMPROVEMENT

Despite the fact that other researchers often document inconsistency between teachers' beliefs and teaching practices (Fang, 1996; Richardson, 1996), my research revealed consistencies between teacher beliefs and practice. After conducting life history interviews with six teachers in two urban K–8 schools, observing two teachers in their classrooms on a weekly basis, and conducting five teacher study groups with the six teachers, I was able to map backgrounds and beliefs onto instructional practices. I documented *critical incidents*, events that remained with participants and held meaning beyond the momentary interaction, as part of my classroom observations by focusing on five focal students in each classroom and their interactions with the teacher. Critical incidents represent an alternative way to capture participants' stories; the meaning ascribed to an event that reveals a view of self may provide a window into the possibilities of future actions (Query, Kreps, Arneson, & Caso, 2001).

In the study group, teachers presented critical incidents from interactions with students in their classroom in order to reflect on these exchanges, develop a deeper understanding about what informed teachers' actions, and better understand the motivations behind a student's choices. This reflection and the insights from colleagues led to new strategies, likely to improve future exchanges. One example worth noting occurred during our final study group session, when I was presenting findings related to how teachers thought about teaching across difference. One of the White female teachers said she felt that even though she spent greater time with the students on a daily basis, the Black female cafeteria workers had an easier time connecting to her students, presumably because of their race. Interestingly, two of the Black female teachers from another school, remarked that, in their experience, shared racial background did not automatically foster an easier connection between the teachers and their students. This assumption is one that is shared by other educators. My colleague, Anita Chikkatur, and I interrogated the belief that researchers (or teachers) who share social identities will make immediate connections with youth (Chikkatur & Jones-Walker, 2013). The context of the study group was a space where a conversation among teachers upended this belief, when a Black female teacher discussed the strategies that she had to employ to build a relationship with her students, even though there were numerous similarities in their respective backgrounds.

The influences of the teacher study group on participants' beliefs and practice support Drake et al.'s (2001) conclusion that the critical incidents method tends to uncover systems of beliefs that are more closely aligned with instructional practice than those that surface through traditional interviews, most likely because there is less distance between professed beliefs and beliefs that drive actions. In addition, the fact that teacher participants in this study group constantly participated in reflection about how their identities related to instructional decisions most likely increased the consistency between beliefs and practices. In the moments when espoused beliefs did not line up with teacher practice, it was often because a teacher was trying to maintain a sense of efficacy in an unforgiving environment. An example was discussed in Chapter 3 when Andrea Carter refers to her students as lazy but later reflects that they are just young people, who may need more direction and support than she had imagined. Andrea's initial response emerged from her frustration with students' behavior and was an attempt to motivate her class to take on additional responsibility for their work.

Focusing on critical incidents revealed that reflective practitioners engaged students partly because they were confident in their ability to connect to students across difference. I have established that beliefs are the driver of action; therefore, if teachers articulate similar goals, but have vastly different ideas about connecting with students and reaching learners, their interactions and pedagogy will be different. For example, even though the majority of teachers in the study group believed that talking with students about inequity would make learning more relevant and purposeful to them, the manner in which these conversations unfolded differed significantly from one teacher to another. There were four teachers (of the six) who consistently articulated the importance of recognizing differences when teaching across cultural boundaries; three of those four teachers viewed diversity as a positive contribution to the teaching experience, and one teacher saw it as a constraint. In part because of the dissonance from the competing ideas, the two teachers who suggested race/ethnicity and culture were not necessarily important features of the teaching and learning process also tended to make statements suggesting that the recognition of difference was, in fact, important. When one of the two teachers did endorse the importance of recognizing difference, he talked about how the diversity of race, class, and perspective benefitted instruction and learning.

Change in practice was not simply about taking stock of one's instruction; reflection on, and awareness of, the self was one of the keys to effective practice. When interactions are left unexamined, teacher practices also tend to go unexamined; therefore new pedagogical strategies cannot develop. Teachers sharing critical incidents in the cross-school study group provided a common text that was an essential feature in teasing out teacher identities and goals from the identities and goals of students. Without this concrete tool many of the nuances of language that revealed teachers' systems of beliefs would have remained invisible and uninterrogated. For example, when there were clear commonalities in teachers' classroom goals, the majority of teachers talked about this role as identifying students' assets and facilitating the construction of knowledge. Two teachers, who were aware of how social inequities shaped students' lives and frequently limited young people's access to quality educational experiences, occasionally felt that too great a barrier existed between themselves and the learners they instructed since they were unable to understand the students' experiences. In their minds, difference in race/ethnicity, age, and gender were barriers to developing a relationship with the students, which in turn affected how their teaching impacted these students. It is easy to agree upon goals, in the abstract, but the concrete examples from daily practice provided clear cases for teachers to interrogate, with specificity, how the understanding of identities, beliefs, discourse, and goals were enacted. When teachers shared classroom incidents, they often brought up complex issues that sometimes surfaced more disagreement, challenging individuals' ideas about the most appropriate response or goal.

Can Teacher Inquiry Make the Difference?

Teacher inquiry groups are a venue for identity-work to happen; they provide a space for teachers to reflect on their instructional practice and interactions with students. These groups can also help teachers map how their backgrounds and beliefs inform teaching decisions. The cross-racial, cross-school teacher study group surfaced important implications for practice related to how collaborative teacher talk can support the negotiation of educational mandates. If teacher learning communities are populated by trusted colleagues, a space can be forged where teachers bring their entire selves and professional judgments to the educational project. Discussions, examination of practice, and analyses of critical incidents that occurred in the teacher study group proved to be the primary vehicle for shifting teacher beliefs and practices.

School structures and the demands on teachers' time often disrupt the possibility for regular and sustained inquiry among teachers. Too often professional development sessions resemble full staff meetings, where new mandates and policies are explained. These meetings typically take on a "training paradigm" (Little, 1993) where an outside "expert" presents new practices expected to improve school efficiency and student outcomes. If districts dedicated as much professional development time to effectively improving pedagogical practice, where teachers would set the agenda, share instructional assignments, or pose problems of practice (Lampert, 1985), there would be a vast improvement in teaching practice, given the fact that less structured interaction among colleagues is a critical element of improvement (Parise & Spillane, 2010). Teachers would have the opportunity to engage in the activities which are at the core of their work—designing lessons, teaching, and looking at student work in order to engage in an ongoing assessment of students to inform their practice. One teacher observed that "we would get started on these really rich conversations and have to stop abruptly. I know I wasn't able to make a few [meetings] but if we did these like every other Thursday, I would just die to have these kinds of conversation in a mixed teacher study group about difference" (personal communication, June 12, 2006). These spaces can support and nurture teachers at the same time that they provide a venue to develop new strategies for instruction.

As is the case with any structural reforms, the districtwide implementation of inquiry groups has had varying results. Over the past decade districts have instituted a variety of structures with the goal of improvement. These include mandatory grade-level team meetings focused on collaboratively examining student work, and cross-grade teams (e.g., Teaching and Learning Collaborative in San Diego). In addition, school-based and cross-school inquiry groups have proliferated (e.g., National Writing Project Teacher Inquiry Communities, Coalition for Essential Schools, National School Reform Faculty's Critical Friends Groups). Such teacher learning communities (TLCs) are teacher driven but typically require the support—time, resources, respect for teacher expertise—of administrators. A range of gains related to teacher quality have been cited that result from teacher learning groups: bridging practice and research, addressing problems of retention, linking teacher practice and content area, fostering transformative teaching, and improving learning.

The Role of Leadership in Transforming School Cultures

The Boston Pilot School Network, where autonomous district schools were created, was successful in part because of school- and district-level leadership. Leaders at school and district levels must establish norms of trust that translate to a collective responsibility for student learning. Bryk and colleagues (1999) have established that collaborative work is more likely to occur and produce change in pedagogical practice when school leaders create a community of trust and collaboration. In such school contexts teachers are granted more autonomy so that they are able to innovate in the context of their classrooms and as leaders in their school community. Leadership, not directives, is critical for embedding this professional practice into a school community in a way that enhances teacher learning. Educational researchers have argued for decades about the importance of setting aside time for teacher collaboration (see Darling-Hammond & McLaughlin, 1995; Little, 1982), yet the strategies for teacher learning and educational reforms rarely are incorporated into state and federal education policies, although the state of Vermont stands as one exception to this pattern (Parise & Spillane, 2010).

The reality that standards, newly adopted curriculum, and accountability are the barriers to improved pedagogy is ironic. If school leaders and teachers were granted more autonomy, these constraints would be minimized and collaborative inquiry could be supported. The power and value of teachers working together on established goals and critical questions is harnessed when initiated by and owned by teachers. The knowledge that results from this "teacher work" can and should inform school practices and decisionmaking.

Although school change models often require all members of the staff to participate in an improvement initiative, how educators are brought on board in these improvement efforts is as important as the strategy for reform. Seven out of 15 midcareer teachers who joined the Urban Teachers Leadership Institute reported that their school administrators did not support their efforts at leadership, did not typically value teacher leaders, and/ or occasionally asked for teacher input but were not particularly supportive of teachers once it was provided (Tamir, 2013). Therefore, it is not surprising that despite the proliferation of teacher learning communities (also referred to as professional learning communities, or PLCs), systemic change in teacher practice or improved learning outcomes is yet to be realized. However, this does not mean it cannot be achieved. Instead, policymakers should consider the following questions:

- What is the larger environment for implementation?
- How do school-based administrators (instructional leaders) lead?
- What are the mechanisms for accountability (are they only external and punitive)?
- Are teachers treated as experts in their fields and viewed as capable of improving?
- Are students viewed as capable of performing high-level intellectual work?

The interest, influence, and potential that the teacher study group represents is encouraging because of the replicability of this structure for professional development, through reflection on teaching exchanges and identity-making. The opportunity for teachers to share and reflect on their interactions in the classroom informed beliefs and actions. Previous research has pointed to the intractability of teacher beliefs (see Nespor, 1987), but as teacher participants in my study struggled to deal with differences and how to most effectively teach students, there was tremendous value in conversing with their colleagues. Richardson (1996) points to the potential of the inquiry process, facilitated by the critical incident method, because it has been shown to enhance and shift teacher belief systems. Bussis and colleagues (1976) discuss how teachers' personal constructs of their students and the curriculum shape their practices. Their research argues that teacher change only occurred if one engaged in "personal exploration, experimentation, and reflection" (p. 17). The activities described by those who research teacher belief systems and argue that interrogating beliefs has the potential to shift practices echo my description of the key elements of teacher identity-work that can lead to sustained pedagogical reform.

SYSTEMATIZING AND SUPPORTING IDENTITY-WORK

It is essential to systematize this work on a larger scale. To many, groups of teachers reflecting on instructional practice may not seem very important or at all rigorous; it is possible that few policymakers would view these interactions as the lynchpin to improving student outcomes. But teacher-based development of practice is the essential tool for improving teaching and learning when focused on student learning outcomes and concerned with documenting the questions, conversations, responses, and impact of practice (Cochran-Smith & Lytle, 2009).

The key barriers to instruction that teachers in two different study groups noted were the rigidity of district curriculum (particularly in mathematics), the frequency of benchmark testing, and the length of state assessments, which significantly decreased instructional time. Teachers also received clear messages that the sole indicator of achievement was test scores, which is not necessarily representative of student learning. As a result of this focus on standardized assessments, prioritizing activities that would increase engagement and deepen the relationship between the teacher and learner, while making connections between curriculum and out-of-school contexts, may seem gratuitous to some. One teacher–leader described time as a primary barrier to promoting critical thinking, contextualized learning, and engaging in caring relationships with his students. A high school mathematics instructor, he stated a primary barrier to his pedagogical practice is "accountability, as it's being currently conceived." For example, he stated that when "teaching the breadth of [geometry] content that students need to do well on that [state] test will absolutely be a limitation on the kinds of constructivist, progressive things that I can do in that class" (personal communication, August 3, 2011). The constraints that practitioners experienced extended beyond the walls of the classroom and informed how staff development time was allocated and what counted as professional development.

Despite the fact that teacher work has been established as deeply personal and connected to individuals' backgrounds and their way of being in the world, the emphasis on identity-work may still be viewed as irrelevant or inconsequential. If we are willing to acknowledge that the act of teaching is directly related to who we are as individuals, then when educational policies, district structures, or school practices limit teacher decisionmaking and constrain instructional practices, it necessarily forecloses on the possibility that teachers will perform their responsibilities to the highest standard.

This is not a call to abandon standards but a call to redefine our terms so school systems are more accountable in providing teachers with the conditions in which they can be expected to perform to their greatest potential. Current strategies are frequently concerned with documenting failure and penalizing staff and schools that do not have the resources, time, or conditions to make the changes that are needed. There is ample evidence that teachers are willing to be accountable. Engaging in teacher team meetings and study groups in Boston, Philadelphia, New York, and with regional district teams in the West, has pointed to this fact. In the cross-school study group that is featured in this chapter, successes and challenges were shared in order to collaboratively pose new instructional strategies that might bring about improvements in learning. Educators must be accountable to the communities they serve, which requires knowing the community and engaging members of the community in schooling on their terms.

Redefining accountability, providing more teacher autonomy, and supporting embedded professional development in the form of teacher inquiry groups are the conditions that are necessary for identity-work, which will shift teacher beliefs and lead to instructional change and improved student outcomes. Teacher development and teacher improvement must place on the agenda self-reflection and analysis of one's position vis-à-vis individuals, institutions, and the world.

In the following chapter, I examine the identities of urban public schools as institutions and consider the identities of students and schools and how various institutional types offer, represent, or challenge the promise of a high-quality public education that produces engaged citizens. Current federal policy and local neoliberal practices appear to threaten the very existence of a purely public educational system.

CHAPTER 6

Identities of U.S. Public Education

The theory of democracy and education that then prevailed [in the 1950s] was informed by conceptions of social homogeneity, simplicity, and an overarching common identity of Whiteness rather than social diversity, complexity, and multiple identities.

—J. D. Anderson (2001, p. 130)

Despite the amount of attention and resources that recently have been directed toward improving public schools and the increased role of the federal government, it appears that there is actually little interest in providing good educational options for poor children of color. On June 13, 2014, Robert Reich, former U.S. Secretary of Labor, cited a study that revealed that the United States is one of three "advanced" nations that spend less on poor children than on wealthier youth. It is ill conceived to imagine that students who have the least resources and the most social, psychological, and medical challenges should be assigned the least in terms of qualified teachers (Darling-Hammond & Berry, 2006), functioning facilities, sufficient materials, and varied course offerings, yet be expected to compete as well as their middle- and upper-class peers. New educational policies are framed as interventions that will produce more equitable schools, yet in communities across the country we have seen decreasing state budgets and urban school districts that are unable to make payroll or are uncertain of how they will have the funds to open the doors for the upcoming academic year.

Reich (2014) argues that politicians advance three big mistruths about poverty, because it is far cheaper than addressing the real solutions: "good-paying jobs, adequate safety nets, and excellent schools." The political establishment would prefer the public to believe that economic growth and additional jobs reduce poverty rather than increased wages and job security; they also propose a singular solution to reducing poverty: changing the behaviors and ambitions of poor people. This logic has been a popular explanation for failing schools for the last 40-plus years; it is a "culture of poverty" argument that suggests students and families must change their behaviors and orientation toward school in order to be more successful. The poor are cast as people of color who are undeserving and lazy members of American society, who do not value education or work (Lipman, 2011) when, in fact, it is often the high expectations that community members hold about what school can and should offer that informs peoples' dissatisfaction about the poor quality of district schools in urban communities.

The first chapters of this book focused on identity-work in the context of classrooms, teacher communities, and schools. In this chapter, I focus on how discourses about public education construct an identity for public schools that contributes to their failure. The examples of teacher practice and professional communities of teachers described in previous chapters demonstrate that school reform policies are designed to fail because they leave little space for critical elements of teaching and learning. Current reform policies tend to depress instructional rigor and student engagement. The sociopolitical context must be considered, if our aim is to reverse these trends, because a great deal is at stake for the identity of public education and its very existence.

I spoke with a middle-class Caribbean American mother, after viewing the documentary *Waiting for Superman* (Birtel & Guggenheim, 2010). She was a graduate of New York City schools, having attended a special admissions high school, and went on to earn her doctorate in education at an Ivy League institution. We shared many similarities: racial and ethnic identities, class background, educational background, and our professional contexts—but the narrative of the film had opposite impacts on us. She was so disturbed by the statistics and documentation of conditions for learning that she felt even more justified in sending her children to a prestigious private school in the suburbs.

My reaction to the film included anger and frustration about how persuasively school choice and, more specifically, charter schools are presented without acknowledging alternative innovations (e.g., in-district charters, improving neighborhood schools, more equitable funding formulas) or the negative effect that this particularly strategy has had on public school systems. Going to see the film and engaging in conversations about it was presented by publicists (and filmmakers) as a social action that would save the "failing U.S. education system." I was bothered by the notion that citizens must sit around and wait for a miracle to happen if they hoped for better school options across the board. The limited set of responses seemed to boil down to three choices: (1) Do nothing and wait for a miracle; (2) abandon public schools; or (3) unanimously and uncritically support charter schools. Ironically, school choice is only a strategy in contexts overrun by poor educational choices. Advocates of choice have argued that it is unfair to deny families in failing districts better options for their children because other families can elect to send their children to parochial or private institutions (consider, for example, Black Alliance for Educational Options). Although persuasive at first, this argument is problematic because the choices offered (in the form of vouchers, charters, or specialized district schools) are not the kinds of choices proposed for all communities—they are most prevalent in neighborhoods composed of people of color and poor children. Lotteries for many charter schools and other desirable public schools in cities do not move us toward equality because despite the lottery, families with access to highly sought after charter schools still tend to have more resources and social capital than the average parent.

While the message of *Waiting for Superman* is misdirected, this film and others (e.g., *The Lottery*, Ashman & Sackler, 2010) challenge common narratives that suggest parents in city schools do not participate in or properly value their child's education. The intense competition for high-quality classroom seats in urban centers proves this to be a fallacy. Organizations and public officials who support school choice have used this data to demonstrate the unwavering public support for charters as the best approach to offering better schooling options. During the 2014 national meeting of the American Educational Research Association (http://convention2.allacademic.com/one/aera/aera14/index.php?cmd=Online+Program+View+Event&selected_box_id=161300&PHPSESSID=5pf2ik6jt2653a0vqgushgts20), Robin Lake, Director of the Center for Reinventing Public Education, made an argument about the success and desirability of portfolio models and choice. A Philadelphia scholar of urban studies and an advocate of public education, Elaine Simon said, "No, good neighborhood schools is what families want, not choice." In the absence of quality neighborhood schools, a decent charter school is preferable to deteriorating buildings, understaffed schools, and rigid curricula and accountability structures. Despite the rhetoric of equality that has surrounded recent national reforms, the attempt to improve city schools has been flawed from the beginning. The question we might pose is whether this is a real goal and if the political will exists to accomplish the task. Instead, it appears to be a diversionary tactic or feigned interest. Excessive discussion about improving the education system, instead of creating wide-scale reform, allows public schooling to be intentionally and systematically dismantled.

The national spotlight has been on failing students and the gap in performance between the rich and the poor, between White students and students of color, and between recent immigrants and students whose families have resided in the United States for several generations. It is as though the media attention and the political debate about the best methods for creating highly effective schools is evidence that it is an authentic goal of the country's leadership and a shared desire of the American public. In fact, the focus on failure reinforces negative beliefs about whether students in specific social identity groups can succeed. It highlights the differences between groups and erases the differences within them. In addition, this framing obscures the material and structural conditions that produce gaps in opportunity leading to differential outcomes (Welner & Carter, 2013). The way the conversation is framed reinforces a belief that the time, efforts, and resources dedicated to improving public education systems, particularly in urban contexts, are wasted because failure among particular groups is inevitable.

Framing public education as a failure encourages the public to curtail improvement efforts and distracts from the social and economic problems that plague the system (Anyon, 2005). Unless this discourse is challenged and reframed in a way that accounts for the obstacles facing students, families, and educators, then schools—arguably the most essential public institution—will not only fail to improve, they may cease to exist. Noguera (2003) reminds us that even the most deplorable public schools in impoverished neighborhoods offer a modicum of safety, stability, and—in a handful of cases—opportunities for students. While this is an unsatisfactory threshold, it is important to consider that public institutions, particularly good schools, are something to which all residents of this country should have access. Noguera argues that "the lack of a concerted and sustained effort to respond to failing urban public schools can be explained only by understanding that United States simply does not care that large numbers of children from inner-city schools and neighborhoods are not properly educated" (p. 14). Many of the remedies proposed in the last 5 to 10 years undermine the possibility for systemic change, while providing politicians and the private sector with a platform to claim that they have made every attempt to improve underperforming schools and systems, from state takeovers, school turnarounds, the No Child Left Behind Act, and Common Core, to increased school choice in the form of vouchers, charter schools, and educational management organizations.

Educators, education policymakers, and citizens must reclaim their right to speak about and for public education in a way that leads rather than responds to the misleading conversation within the current terms of the debate. Although local organizing efforts propose counter-solutions to popular strategies such as privatization, choice, standardization, and external management, these local efforts are fractured and silenced and, to date, have lacked the power to shift the national education discourse.

U.S. EDUCATION—INCLUSION AND EXCLUSION

From the inception of schooling in the United States, the identity of the nation was revealed by who was included and who was excluded in the education system. Despite the diverse collection of schools that were available to families with resources—private, public, charitable, for profit, parochial, and sectarian—by the 1890s, 9 of 10 pupils attended public schools (Mondale & Patton, 2001) a ratio that is consistent with the rate of public school attendance today. Although by the mid-20th century, universal access to schooling in the United States outpaced all other countries (Ravitch, 2011), race, class, gender, nationality, and religion were the social categories that continued to determine who had access to quality schools and who did not.

As people from a wider variety of socioeconomic backgrounds, racial and ethnic groups, and national origins were incorporated into the public education system, schools became increasingly stratified, first by school and later by a dual system demarcated by race. Historically, North Americans used segregated schools to ensure that high-quality schools and curriculum were available for the most powerful, and lower-quality schools were intended for immigrants, poor people, and people of color. Problematizing the notion of democracy and education in the quote that begins this chapter, Anderson (2001) also points out that "when you look at the curricula that was developed—domestic science for women, industrial education for African Americans, boarding school for Native Americans—much of what developed under the guise of a democratic and differentiated curriculum was in fact a way to reinforce the kind of class, gender, and race prejudice that existed in society" (pp. 112–113).

While elementary and secondary education in North America was more accessible than in many other nations, and this access led to greater social mobility at the turn of the century, such stories in this era are more often the exception than the rule. This is important to note because of how U.S. citizens perceive educational access and the potential to work hard, receive a good education, and move up the economic ladder. While this scenario may have been part of the early history of the American educational system, it is not a trend that has continued after court-mandated desegregation.

The 1954 *Brown v. Board of Education* case set a course for desegregation, and after the *Brown II* ruling in 1955 ordering schools to integrate "with all deliberate speed," schools slowly and reluctantly desegregated across lines of race and class. It was the 1964 Civil Rights Act, with its monetary incentives to districts that brought the most sweeping change toward the desegregation of schools (Clotfelter, 2011). Despite the persistence of segregated housing and the advent of suburbanization (Massey & Denton, 1993), the percentage of students of color who were incorporated into previously all-White schools grew between 1960 and 1980 but then slowed in the 1990s when the Supreme Court began to authorize the termination of desegregation plans (Orfield, Siegel-Hawley, & Kucsera, 2014).

It is widely understood that despite the rescinding of *de jure* segregation, schools and other institutions experienced *de facto* segregation due to social codes, exclusionary institutional culture, housing patterns, and unofficial policies and practices. Still, a 20-year trend toward desegregated schools has been observed, but now some scholars have argued that U.S. schools have resegregated in the last few decades, beginning in the early 1990s. Resegregation is evidenced by the fact that the 2000 Isolation Index matched the Isolation Index of the 1960s (Clotfelter, 2011; Orfield, Siegel-Hawley,

& Kucsera, 2014; Reardon, Grewal, Kalogrides, & Greenberg, 2012). The 2000 Isolation Index is also described as a measure of segregation of activities among two or more social identity groups. Clotfelter (2004) uses the degree of interracial contact to analyze patterns of segregation in schools. Fiel (2013) argues that there is equal or more racial balance today, but the declining presence of Whites in schools is caused by national demographic shifts. The charter school movement promised better quality schools and increased access to good school options for poor communities and communities of color. Charters have been imagined as public institutions that can be more diverse, more innovative, and more academically rigorous than traditional district schools. Despite this expectation, demographic data show that charter schools have led to an increase in racial segregation because families with social capital choose schools based upon the match between the enrolled students and their own background, power, and status (Belfield & Levin, 2009; Fuller & Elmore, 1996).

A NEW IDENTITY FOR PUBLIC SCHOOLS

The esteem that U.S. citizens hold for public education and the identity of public schools has shifted dramatically over the past 60 years. It is no coincidence that a key turning point of the public sentiment regarding the importance of the U.S. education system corresponds with the *Brown v. Board* ruling and ensuing legal actions, including the 1968 *Green v. Kent* decision, which ended separate state-sanctioned school systems by ruling the freedom of choice plans as unconstitutional. It is ironic that while it was widely understood in the late 1960s that if school options were left to people in the majority culture, this would always lead to segregation and inequality of opportunity, yet in the last decade choice has been seen as a remedy for access to quality schooling. Today, the political establishment and public officials lack a commitment to improving and sustaining the public education system, perhaps because the old mechanisms for stratification (e.g., Jim Crow laws) no longer exist and other strategies (stratification by neighborhood, housing discrimination) were prohibited because of federal policies put in place post–*Brown v. Board*. As a result of federal policies implemented in the mid 1950s to early 1960s, it became harder to exclude minorities, females, or immigrants, or to differentiate opportunities to the degree that this had occurred in previous generations. Given these legislative changes, public schools were unable to serve the interests of the most privileged citizens in the manner in which they did prior to the civil rights movement. As practices and policies became more consistent across communities, "this homogenization of schools has been countered by pressures to reassert differentiation" (Belfield & Levin, 2009, p. 513) through districtwide magnet schools, vocational or themed schools, and, more recently, school choice. Reforms that fall under this umbrella include charter schools, voucher programs, or tuition tax credit that reduces tax burdens for paying private school tuitions. New mechanisms for stratification developed in the form of neoliberal policies (e.g., marketization) that tout a goal of increasing equity and access, yet penalize and threaten those schools and districts that are most vulnerable.

Reimagining Cities and Schools

In the *New Political Economy of Urban Education: Neoliberalism, Race, and the Right to the City*, Lipman (2011) defines *neoliberalism* as "an ensemble of economic and social policies, forms of governance and discourses and ideologies that promote individual self-interest, unrestricted flow of capital, deep reductions in the cost of labor, and sharp retrenchment of the public sphere" (p. 6). Lipman argues that the goal of the neoliberal project is to change not only how we think about the world, but also our subjectivities. In the neoliberal project, the role of cities is central; therefore remaking cities is a critical step in reframing the identities of the U.S. public. In neoliberal governance, large social policies (e.g., education) are redefined, and with this comes a redefinition of who we are as individuals and what we should value. The motivation to remain a global leader and offer top-notch public education to all citizens, as was the case at the start of the 20th century, seems to have dissipated. Today, the public sector is abandoned for those with meager resources, while it is privatized to earn a profit for those who have already amassed significant wealth.

U.S. leaders' (public officials, business leaders, politicians) concept of schooling has fundamentally shifted from an institution of government sponsorship to an entity led by the competitive marketplace. If ever there was an investment in creating a nation where hard work, good grades, and perseverance could catapult one to the elite class (Reich, 2012), that is no longer the case. In the new conceptualization, what is viewed as the bureaucracy and ineffectiveness of schools is replaced by efficiency and innovation through consumer choice. Although little evidence has supported the merit of marketplace approaches to education, and studies show that there are little to no improvements in academic achievement of charter school students (Belfield & Levin, 2009; Center for Research on Education Outcomes, 2013), the U.S. Department of Education has shown overwhelming support of this venture. For example, a stated intention of the Race to the Top grant announced in 2009 was to deliver a more competitive market to the public through the creation of more high-performing charter schools. Advocates of a market-based model highlight the importance of parental choice and overlook the fact that a key facet for efficiency and improvement is community and parental voice. In fact, the opportunity for students to exit schools may undermine the likelihood of exerting pressure on school leaders or education managers to make necessary changes (Belfield & Levin, citing Hirschman, 1970). Previously, parents and community board members exerted pressure on schools and districts to address issues or inadequacies that were identified. In a market-based approach, parents assume that there is more power in leaving the school community than fighting for necessary improvements. This type of accountability does not lead schools to improve; it leads schools to flounder and become forced to close their doors.

In a cohesive democracy the purpose of schools has historically been to educate and produce engaged citizens, not solely to meet individual needs and interests. The notion of education as a common social good has been eroded by the recasting of citizens as consumers of schooling rather than citizens who have the right to high-quality education (Lipman, 2011) without regard to their identities or ZIP codes. The only true beneficiaries of a market-based approach to education are businesses, including education consultants. A multimillion-dollar industry has been created to "improve" schools, yet very little change has occurred in the conditions of schooling or in student outcomes. Private dollars dedicated to public schooling have increased significantly, but the funds have flowed to testing agencies, textbook companies, for-profit management organizations, and education intermediaries. The Bill and Melinda Gates Foundation invested $160 million to fund the creation of the Common Core State Standards and is now partnering with Pearson to develop K–12 curricula aligned with the Common Core, and two federally funded multistate consortia (Partnership for Assessment of Readiness for College and Careers, and Smarter Balanced Assessment) are developing assessments at the cost of $350 million.

It is difficult to understand these enormous expenditures that have borne few results when many educators understand the necessary conditions, cost, pedagogies, curricula, and supports that are required to create effective urban schools. There have been a plethora of examples of successful school models such as the MET School in Providence, RI, Central Park East in New York City, Fenway High in Boston, and the Auto Academy at West Philadelphia High (now the Workshop School). There are fewer successful districtwide models, and these examples tend to yield results that are hard to sustain, particularly with leadership transitions, as was the case with NYC Community School District 2, led by Tony Alvarado, and in the San Diego School District under Alan Bersin with Alvardo as his Chancellor (Ravitch, 2011). Chicago Public Schools also boasted significant gains until the departure of Paul Vallas in 2001. In 2006, Boston Public Schools was recognized for being the urban school district that demonstrated the most improvement in the country under the leadership of Thomas Payzant.

The autonomy extended to teachers and school leaders was a key condition of success for each of these schools and districts. Although I already explored this initiative in Chapter 4, here I want to draw the distinction between autonomous district schools and urban charter schools. Many districts now provide greater choice to families (e.g., Philadelphia's diverse provider model), and although charter schools offer parental choice and typically grant more freedom, they are not the only way to increase autonomy for teachers and educational leaders. Pilot schools and other districts that offer autonomy to a cadre of schools provide an array of schooling options, but the theory of change is different from portfolio models that have led to the proliferation of charters. Autonomy means that the expertise, located at the school site, can be brought to bear on key instructional decision and school policies. School choice is expected to improve educational options because failing schools will close and good schools will emerge. This approach to improvement could lead to entire school districts being comprised of charter schools (Chester Upland School District in Pennsylvania was majority charter school district in 2006 before a new Empowerment Board was appointed).

School choice and the Common Core State Standards Initiative (CCSSI) represent two neoliberal approaches to improvement. Initially, CCSSI benefited from the support of parents, school administrators, and powerful teachers unions because the Common Core represented better, smarter standards; more student-centered teaching; and increased expectations for students (Karp, 2013). However, the situation has drastically changed. In January 2014 the largest teachers union in New York State decided to withdraw support for the CCSSI and they took a vote of "no confidence" in the Commissioner of Education (Karp, 2013). Although educators, students, and families welcomed new high-quality standards, they became disconcerted by how these standards were implemented and the accountability structures that accompanied them. These policies contribute to the deprofessionalization of teaching because the directives transfer decisions about curriculum, pedagogy, and assessment away from teachers into the hands of academics, political officials, and representatives of testing companies, who were the primary architects of the Common Core. At the same time, these policies undermined the possibility that students will feel capable and can demonstrate high levels of success, because of the increased challenge, the fast-paced implementation, and the punitive consequences if students and teachers do not meet success.

The top-down nature of the Common Core State Standards Initiative, like the policies that preceded it, suggests that education policy will remain in the hands of the wealthy and powerful and that key decisionmaking about how to improve public education is unlikely to return to educators and engaged citizens. Many people hoped that CCSSI would signal a positive change from the era of No Child Left Behind because it would offer more rigorous standards and a departure from "teaching to the test." The nature of implementation has bred suspicion and frustration. Many educators and activists identify the policy as part of a larger corporate reform strategy, focused more on business and political interest than on improving students' educational experiences (Karp, 2013). By changing how schools are structured and who designs education policies and practices, the institution of schooling is fundamentally different from the past. Once the structure and design of a public institution has shifted, the next stage in neoliberal policymaking is to create new markets for the consolidation of capital; we have witnessed the proliferation of markets (e.g., testing, curriculum, professional development, school and district management) brought about by federal initiatives, such as NCLB, and expanded through the Race to the Top and CCSS Initiatives.

The Purpose of Schooling

The U.S. school system is no longer a critical feature in the nation's democracy. The opening quote by historian James Anderson (2001) suggests that the goal and purposes of schooling changed as the country's heterogeneity increased and the mechanisms for stratifying groups, based on social identity, were written out of the law. The democratic nature of schooling, espoused by Jefferson and put into practice by Dewey, was not expected to extend to all members of society (Perkinson, 1968). The utility and value of schools integrating, civilizing, and Americanizing new immigrants during the early 1900s dissipated, similar to the federal government's waning commitment to desegregating unified school districts in the 1990s. In addition, the ideological tide in the United States has shifted away from the ideals of a democratic society with a commitment to the common good, and has returned to principles of Social Darwinism prevalent in the late-19th century (Reich, 2012). These theories are enacted in neoliberal policies, favoring noninterventionist practices of the state in support of competitive markets. Such policies increase authority and wealth for the most powerful and decrease resources and power for the most vulnerable. This ideological and economic shift has manifested in a new identity and purpose for U.S. public schools. Urban schools, serving mostly poor and minority students, are now viewed as a marketplace, where business interests reign over teaching, learning, and preparing future citizens for a democracy.

To reverse the discourse about urban schools, to ensure that schools are reasonably funded rather than continually defunded, and to safeguard the existence of public school districts into the next decade, the American public must offer critical support to urban public education systems. Local organizing efforts must join forces with campaigns in other cities to create a national campaign. A greater percentage of the American public must become aware that the existence of the public school system is at stake, particularly in cities. To take no action while the system devolves will make the public complicit in the failure of the democratic ideal of public schooling. A plethora of images, articles, and documentaries have drawn a clear picture of the challenges and conditions students in urban communities face. These representations have seared into people's consciousness the extraordinary gap that exists between poor students of color and their White middle- and upper-middle-class counterparts. The current remedy has been to document the gap and penalize young people for the system's failings rather than highlight how such a gap in achievement can occur (Darling-Hammond, Newton, & Wei, 2013). The nature of neoliberal discourse allows the average U.S. citizen to believe that they are not implicated in the rampant failure or inequality in the system. This framing justifies political and personal choices, as well as ideological beliefs, that may contribute to the gap in opportunities. The status quo in many school settings provides ample evidence for a family's rationale for leaving district schools in cities (for private, parochial, suburban, and charter schools) rather than motivating groups to ensure that no children will have to endure unconscionable conditions and an absence of opportunities for learning. The limited options and the possibility that parents must jeopardize the health, well-being, and education of their child, if they commit to supporting city schools, leads to a binary framing of the challenge as one must leave public educational systems or suffer.

EDUCATING IN THE 21ST CENTURY

What does the shifting educational discourse and political maneuvering mean for teachers, students and schools? Is it even possible to focus our energies on the identity-making of teachers and students in the process of teaching and learning? We must think about how identities are constructed through pedagogy, practice, and policy at every level of school reform. In reflecting on the greater social and political context of education broadly, and urban education specifically, it is possible to recognize that in order to create authentic sustainable improvements in what students learn and how they perform, the work must occur on a larger political stage. The processes and practices of identity-work may look slightly different on this stage; it may resemble community organizing aimed at shifting the national discourse around education and curtailing new educational policies and local mandates.

One clear step that can be taken is building on the tremendous work of organizers in cities all over the United States (e.g., Chicago's Teachers Union, Philadelphia Student Union and Youth United for Change) including coalitions of parents and community groups, who have protested for a greater allocation of state dollars to fill in the deficits that city schools are carrying due to extreme budget cuts. The phone calls and letters to public officials ought to be taken seriously; the protest in cities and state capitals should not be ignored. More important, although teaching and learning will undoubtedly be altered by federal reforms and national discourse, we must also be sure to design reforms and the conditions for instruction that will allow for students to be known to teachers and for teachers to bring their entire self and their professional judgment to bear in pedagogical decisions.

Whom public schools serve and the purpose of education has changed dramatically in the last 50 years. While the United States has prided itself on being the "land of opportunity," where members of society who work hard, demonstrate success in school, and show tenacity can have access to the best schools, jobs, and a range of opportunities to attain wealth, this is becoming further and further from the truth. The commitment to investing in the public welfare that became popular in the 1920s with the advent of social security, unemployment insurance, labor laws, and a minimum wage was replaced with a belief that the wealthy should be rewarded and that no safety nets are needed for the poor because it would enable irresponsibility (Reich, 2012).

Despite the fact that 90% of U.S. residents attend public schools, it appears that the public is disinterested in the notion of equitable education. It is critical to note that in urban districts, only 5% of White residents enroll in public schools. This figure has decreased with the introduction of charter schools, serving about 5% of the school-aged population. The divestment in equal and accessible quality public education is related to the need to create new mechanisms for stratification, to ensure White privilege and class privilege. Neoliberal strategies have provided the language and rationale, while preserving a sense of what has come to be known as core American values—democracy and freedom. In the new terms, *democracy* has come to be represented by an ability to choose what is best, and *freedom* has been translated to one's freedom to consume and pursue the best for one's individual self (Lipman, 2011, p. 10). This has fundamentally changed the landscape of public education, and I believe it is critical to challenge the new terms and create an authentic commitment to educational equity.

CHAPTER 7

Conclusion

During the course of this book, I have moved from documenting the individual identities of students and teachers and illustrating how background and experience inform beliefs, engagement, and practices in schooling to taking up how teacher identities and perceptions of students' identities inform their curricular decisions. By tracing the importance of identity to education and learning, one can construct implications for practice at a variety of levels, starting from the individual to society. Identity-work is a critical lever for change at every level, but the nature and shape of this work will present itself differently as one moves from the context of the classroom, to the school, to the school district, to the nation at large. A long-term view of the values and purpose of public schooling rounds out the picture and can hopefully sharpen our predictions about the impact of current policies and practices for the future of public education. If it is the case that increasing demographic diversity of the attendees of public schools in the United States complicates some citizens' beliefs about the importance of public schools, then the claim that urban school reform may have failure as an element of its design has veracity. It is attributable to ambivalence about the goal of ensuring that each member of our society has equal access to quality education and jobs with a living wage.

Employing microlevel research that examines identity-making and student experiences in classrooms in order to address the missing link in improvement efforts runs the risk of not persuading crucial audiences such as educational policymakers. In the current era, educational policy has primarily considered quantitative and mixed method studies that rely on standardized test scores as the measure for student achievement. This quantitative approach has narrowed definitions of student learning and the desired outcomes (Orfield, 2009), and has limited the range of strategies for increasing student engagement and learning. For identity-work at the level of the school community and classroom to take hold in a sustained way, federal, state, and district policies must change. The approach I am proposing requires new conceptions of accountability and a system that is designed in a way that captures the complexity of teaching and learning and the needs of multiple stakeholders.

Reflection on experiences and interactions is a key component of identity-making but there is less room for teachers to do this work. In order to support the positive construction of identity, policymakers must design improvement efforts with a belief that individuals are endowed with the capacity to learn at advanced levels and to make adaptations. The belief that when people are offered the appropriate resources, conditions, and supports, they have the potential to achieve success is a critical element to improving public education. If our society focuses on developing human capacity and building partnerships between the government, educators, and parents (Mintrop & Sunderman, 2009), we can usher in new forms of accountability that incentivize talented teachers and all learners.

I am heartened by the overwhelming recognition among public education stakeholders that while NCLB was designed, in theory, to increase equity and access to quality education, it was implemented as a system of quotas and sanctions that imposed impossible requirements. These mandates impeded schools and teachers from doing the work that could make a critical difference in students' lives (Orfield, 2009). This admission supports the core of my argument that the recent course of reform has led to less effective schools and increased student failure. If school districts were redesigned in ways that produced the conditions necessary for schools and teachers to engage in the essential work of learning and understanding students' backgrounds and needs in order to respond to the student population they serve in responsible and thoughtful ways, it would interrupt this trend. The educational reforms that are designed must support creative instruction in the form of polices that leave room for teachers to innovate and offer a curriculum that is rich and meaningful.

Instead of decreasing achievement gaps between poor students and students of color and their more affluent and privileged counterparts, the sanctions imposed by NCLB led to state takeovers, decreased funding for schools, and school closures. With the adoption of NCLB waivers and the creation of the Common Core, an opportunity arose to transition from a basic skills framework toward rigorous interdisciplinary curricula focused on developing conceptual understandings. Unfortunately, the implementation of the Common Core, with its attached accountability structures, is reminiscent of the policies that led to the demise of NCLB. We must completely reframe accountability, creating structures that rely upon multiple measures of students' success, including completing school, acquiring skills for higher education, engaging in relevant and rigorous curriculum, and developing skills needed to be an informed global citizen.

In order for this type of change to occur, citizens must set their sights beyond educational policymaking and rethink federal policy related to housing, health, job development, and services for communities. Instead of producing new markets for wealthy businesses to exploit, we must reinvest in schools and other public institutions. In *Radical Possibilities*, Anyon (2005) persuasively argues that current outcomes are not simply about poorly designed education policies; "failing public schools in cities are, rather, a logical consequence of the U.S. political economy—and the federal and regional policies and practices that support it" (p. 5).

School reform as it is currently conceptualized does not allow space for the insights of community members or for their experiences, and, as a result, these reforms rarely enjoy community support. Teachers, who understand the day-to-day realities of parents' and students' lives and who negotiate daily the challenges of failing schools, poor living conditions, and limited job opportunities, have the opportunity to be key constituents in efforts to create positive and meaningful change in public school systems. Similarly, young people are the most knowledgeable about the conditions of learning, the strained relationships between teachers and students (Gold, Lewis, Suess, Jones-Walker, & Rosen, 2008), and the existence of poor quality instruction in urban schools' contexts (Wilson & Corbett, 2001). As Theresa Perry points out in the introduction to her edited volume, *Quality Education as a Constitutional Right* (Perry et al., 2010), there has been a long history of organizing for better educational options in communities of color and educational activists have turned their attention to enumerating this as a constitutional right of all citizens. She writes, "We have seen the increasing disenfranchisement of local communities in decisions about schools and in discussion about the contents of public education. And as the public sphere has become demonized, so have public schools" (p. xiii).

COMMUNITY-BASED ACTIVISM

In order to challenge the discourse around public education and change the nature and implementation of educational policies, communities must demand something different. The persuasive and seemingly neutral nature of neoliberal practices and the impact of these policies can sometimes feel overwhelming. We must remember that, historically, organized communities have had success in overturning harmful social policy and that the scope of disenfranchisement can be a catalyst for dynamic, thoughtful, and effective collective action. Anyon's (2005) powerful insights should remind all citizens, but especially those working for access to a quality education for all American children, that there is no need to begin anew when planning campaigns for social policy and educational equity; we can draw on the established work of five distinct (and sometimes overlapping) organizing movements: community organizing, educational organizing, youth organizing, progressive labor unions, and living wage campaigns (pp. 154ff).

While acknowledging the importance of affecting policy around labor, housing, job creation, and health care, I will focus on three specific movements and their potential to incite change in campaigns for educational equity. In the previous chapter I asserted that there is the potential for harnessing the energy of local organizing campaigns and developing collective strategies to mobilize public school stakeholders to demand policy changes. In order to arrive at a robust educational policy, funding, and conditions to improve teaching and learning, community, youth and educational organizing must align in collective campaigns to shift educational discourse and change federal policy.

In the summer of 2003 I worked with a team of educators and organizers to plan and facilitate a National Training Institute: Organizing for Educational Excellence. The 12 participating groups were selected from 30 organizations that applied. We worked with four education experts and invited five organizations to present local case studies. Each of the organization that attended the institute had an explicit agenda to mobilize communities in order to improve public schools. Together, the group of more than 100 organizers explored three levels of change: (1) effective strategies for teaching and learning in the classroom; (2) whole-school reform models; and (3) systemwide change, including issues related to standards and accountability. The group was very committed to developing a deeper understanding of the educational landscape and gaining more knowledge about the "technical core" of schooling (Elmore, 2002) in order to strengthen their campaigns. There was tremendous value in having a range of organizing models and a variety of cases from different geographic and political contexts. The presence of groups from across the country produced a vibrant and inspiring conversation across the particulars of our regional borders. These discussions allowed organizers to learn important lessons from their peers and to identify strategies that build upon or contest national reform policies, in order to create better educational experiences for communities across the country.

There is particular promise in youth leading proposed organizing efforts to support educational improvement. For over a decade I served on the board of directors of Youth United for Change, an organization that believes "every young person deserves a quality public education that prepares him or her for success at a four-year university; for a living-wage job; and for active participation in civic life" (see YUC website: youthunitedforchange. org/). While youth organizing is informed by youth development it has a different orientation. Some youth development organizations have shifted from prevention-oriented social service models to building supports for youth and preparing them for adulthood (Lewis-Charp, Yu, & Soukamneuth, 2006). Youth organizing grows out of this framework and provides an integrated approach to social change. Because the organizing work is issued-based, it draws a diverse group of youth coalescing around a common cause. Rather than an attempt to develop skills and civic-mindedness, youth organizing creates spaces for young people to take stock of their environment (e.g., school, community) and identify issues that they feel need to be addressed.

For obvious reasons, public education has been a central part of youth organizing work. In the case of Youth United for Change, committed adults work alongside young people as guides and mentors. Often, youth organizing groups provide social services to support and supplement the inadequate nature of the resources available at school. When young peoples' capacities are developed, their agency is actualized, often in ways that transform their personal identities (Anyon, 2005). Through this process, youth's civic engagement is sparked or buttressed, leading many youth to become social activists. In this way, youth organizing is an out-of-school model for identity-making with peers and adults and in relationship to society at large. The practice of reflecting upon one's experiences and identifying issues that need to be addressed within communities is the very description of identity-work that I have espoused throughout the book. We need to develop similar opportunities in schools, in community groups, and within all settings that young people occupy. We must think about creating these experiences for youth, not only to improve their lives but also the vibrancy of our society as a whole. Our collective outlook on the world will brighten significantly if we keep in mind that young peoples' participation and the learning (academic, political, social) that occurs during their path to adulthood are critical elements in creating the necessary changes in education and the world. If one embraces and facilitates their energy, ideas, and activism, these necessary changes will be upon us.

Initially, Youth United for Change (YUC) focused on an issues-based campaign at each of the five school chapters. Later, YUC began to identify districtwide issues that were affecting students' educational opportunities. In recent years, YUC has been a strong voice in state campaigns to increase school funding in response to budget cuts that have left Philadelphia schools without libraries, nurses, librarians, school counselors, and other essential staff. Their organizing efforts evolved from being school-based to becoming districtwide efforts. In 2005 YUC began to function in collaboration with parent and community organizations to amass power and affect larger-scale changes. It was during this year that YUC successfully won a campaign to restructure three comprehensive neighborhood schools into small autonomous schools (Mediratta, Shah, & McAlister, 2009; Suess & Lewis, 2007).

Tremendous promise is contained in local organizing, but the fact remains that there are over 100 organizing groups in New York City, but only 10% of students enrolled in the city schools are affected by these campaigns (Anyon, 2005); these numbers demonstrate the scope of the problem and the amount of effort that is required for groups of youth activists to have the level of impact equal to the enormity of the challenges that their organizing activities seek to resolve. The numbers also highlight the urgency of unifying various local youth organizing groups because, joined with community and educational efforts, they represent the greatest potential for creating significant policy reform. We have to continue to build the power of strong local organizing projects that are working tirelessly in their communities at the same time that we build coalitions of strong organizations across the country, thereby creating a national unified campaign. Oakes and Rogers (2006) make this point in their concluding chapter of *Learning Power*, suggesting that "movement organizing informed by public inquiry provides our best hope for disrupting the logic of schooling that creates and sustains inequality" (p. 158). The authors caution readers that unless reforms confront the logic of merit, deficit, and scarcity, attaining equality of educational opportunity will be impossible. The logic of merit is framed on the idea that students compete on an equal playing field for educational advantage based on their ability and hard work. A deficit framework rests on the belief that schooling cannot alter the limitations of students' experiences because of poverty, race, culture, or family background. This allows students' lack of educational opportunity to be framed as an individual's failure to strive rather than structural forces consistently constructing barriers to entire communities' efforts to improve student outcomes. Cultural deficit models, joined with logics of merit, lead to theories of scarcity—the idea that only a limited amount of opportunity and resources can be afforded to public education (Oakes & Rogers, 2006).

Educational researchers have previously argued that technical reforms, while changing school structures, standards, or curricula, leave the central beliefs about schooling untouched and therefore improvements are not realized. I have argued throughout this book that current educational reforms are designed to safeguard the status quo while employing an equity discourse that activates the public's fears and self-interest.

IMPLICATIONS

Previously schools were imagined as a great equalizer in society; they were recognized for having the potential to empower students to transform their individual lives and have a positive impact on society. While the meritocratic model has always been a myth, the transformation of the U.S. economy has fundamentally changed the role of schools. Successful completion of high school no longer leads to a living wage nor to the ability to attend college or attain middle-class jobs. It is dangerous to rely on an old model set on an ideal that schools will transform society if this is no longer the case. It is critical to join efforts to enact public policy reform that produces the conditions for the best education reform. Educational reforms that take into account social identities and human capacity will create the policies to enable student and teacher identity-work to become a lynchpin in improving student experiences and academic learning.

This study originated as an examination of the interaction between teachers and students and the coconstruction of identities through daily practice. I imagined how classroom culture—the beliefs/norms, climate, and behaviors—is informed by the identity of learners and teachers through classroom exchanges. While I situated this exploration within the larger institutional, social, historical, and political context, I only hinted at the ways that larger social forces informed microlevel exchanges. Too often our work is isolated in this manner; we consider student identities or teacher identities but not both. We analyze microlevel behaviors and practices or macrostructures. In order for identity-work to support substantial improvements in student learning, we must create the necessary conditions for change at the level of society, national policy arenas, state/district/school policy, and within the context of the classroom. Joining identity-making and educational organizing has the potential to realize these changes.

Afterword

In the past decade I have moved from teaching and learning with middle school students to teaching and learning with teachers, first within a university setting and now within a state department of education. In each of these settings I was referred to in a variety of ways: a "breath of fresh air," or someone who was "out on her own" more often than as a team player. In the classroom it was not unusual to have someone walk in and find me lying on the floor working next to a student. As a state employee, I often find myself talking about mathematics with teachers, with no measureable outcomes in mind except that they will know more mathematics so that when the moment arises, they can share that knowledge with students. It turns out that learning mathematics content is not a measureable outcome that can be documented in a SMART goal. Also, lying on the floor to learn mathematics is not seen as a desirable classroom arrangement when district teams walk through schools. In the university setting there are no examples of my being different because having original thoughts is the expectation, not the exception. I lasted 5 years being a middle school teacher before I was too exhausted and worn down to continue. I am still in my first few months in a state department of education. We will see if I can find ways to be myself, share my best self, and make a difference in this position.

Ten years ago, when this research project began, I did not have the vocabulary for the study of identity. In the midst of the research I felt pressure to get to know my students, their families, their likes and dislikes, and then create curriculum around the things I learned about them. In this realm, I was a fish out of water, or rather a small-town southerner living in the urban Northeast. I was at a distinct disadvantage. What I did not understand intellectually then, or have language to describe, is that I wanted each of my kids to succeed each day. And I knew from my college teaching that meeting success was the key. Once kids succeeded and knew they could succeed, they were motivated to succeed more. I worked tirelessly every day to make that happen, often all night too. I never lost the urgency to reach each and every kid, fearing their loss of opportunities in life if I did not reach them. About a year ago, I was rewarded when I ran into one of my former middle school students on the subway, and she offered, "The best part about your class was that you let us be ourselves." I wish that phrase, that question—"Do your kids feel like they can be themselves in your classroom?"—was being bantered around the hallways, asked in meetings, posted on the walls of the teacher's lounge. But it wasn't, which might be why I began journaling my second or third week of teaching.

Journaling was how I had those hard conversations with myself. And those daily journal entries, made at a coffee shop or on my walk home, always began with the most immediate concerns—those children I had not reached, who usually acted out in a way that let me know that I had not reached them. Gradually, my attention turned to children I did reach and ways to do things differently tomorrow so that I stood a chance of reaching more kids. Sometimes it meant getting one student to sit in a corner with another so she could get him to get his work done while keeping him out of my face because I was at my wits' end with him and just needed a break. He might even learn something with his student colleague, and I could follow up with him later after I got others in the class learning, or even tomorrow or the next day. I never got it all right.

Trying to have these conversations with others often turned to general reasons why a certain student wasn't learning or larger family or societal issues, most of which teachers had no control over, but issues that make great conversations for policymakers. I had decisions to make before the morning, so I needed concrete steps—a way to find one-on-one time with the student, a way to show a concept in a different way, a connection to something he did understand—and I needed them quick. This is not to say that there were no caring conversations about students; there were. But it was not part of the structure of our work to have these conversations, or to learn how to have them. Learning how to have them is perhaps the most crucial piece.

In the intervening 10 years, I spent the majority of my time as a college professor of mathematics education, where research, reflection, and innova-tion are the norm. Courageously trying new ideas and learning from them, which caused such tension in my last year of middle school teaching, was business as usual in the university setting. For the last few months, however, I have worked in a state department of education, and much has changed since I was in the classroom full time. There are many more structures, and the implementation of these structures seems much more rigid than when I was teaching. I am not sure that I would survive even 1 year in some of the schools I work within now, even though when I was teaching my kids made AYP 4 out of those 5 years. In that 5th year I was not able to reach my kids, despite all my efforts. Looking back, I see that there were too many rules to follow. I could not be myself, so I could not reach my kids, and I failed my students. I fear that the majority of classrooms today might be more like this 5th-year experience if I tried to return to teaching now. There seems to be so little wiggle room.

The thing is, I believe in national involvement in education. I come from the rural South where girls took home economics and boys took shop, where White people filled the "A" and "B" groups, which had the best teachers, and people of color filled the "D" and "F" groups, which had the worst teachers. Even as a middle school teacher, I thought the state-mandated assessments were great tests. They presented good, hard mathematics, content worth teaching. I am a fan of the Common Core State Standards for mathematics, and I agree with teaching the structure and the organization of mathematics, not just how to work individual problems in a textbook. And, like the state-mandated test I administered to my students, the PARCC (Partnership for Assessment of Readiness for College and Careers) tests, which are designed to meet the Common Core standards, are good, rigorous mathematics that students need to think through.

So, why is it, now that I am in the field again, working within schools and districts with teachers and students in front of me every day, that I find myself needing to journal again after work? Finding the space and language to have conversations with others has become difficult again. I am not able to just talk mathematics with math teachers and math facilitators despite everyone agreeing that lack of content knowledge is a key issue. I continually am faced with the question of how to fit what I am saying into a structure that has been set up by a district or the state. When I am facilitating sessions with teachers, if I suggest getting mathematical ideas that support students in seeing the structure of mathematics on the classroom walls, teachers respond that discretionary wall space is limited. My visceral reaction to rules and regulations about what can and cannot, or should or should not, be on your walls, is tempered by gratitude that at least I am in a position to talk with administrators about wall space—administrators in the building, in the district, in the state, all of whom are somehow accountable, right up to the federal government.

When I share my excitement about mathematical conversations I am having in schools with colleagues, questions about how I am measuring my success inevitably interrupt my excitement. My reaction to this is again visceral: Get out of my face! Learning takes time! Give us a minute! But of course I do not share this reaction; I simply go home and journal, noting not to share as much in the future, even as I am figuring out ways to sneak in more mathematics under the disguise of mandated classroom routines, curricular development, or while no one is looking. Is it possible to set national goals, national expectations, but then allow for alternate ways to arrive at those goals and expectations, alternate ways to measure progress toward these goals? With each new set of math standards—NCTM standards in 1989 and the Common Core State Standards in 2010—the mathematics education community is asking for higher level thinking about broader ideas, leaving speedy rote manipulations to cheap calculators, but the implementation seems to me more and more micromanaging of the most minor details of the classroom environment. Is it possible to have standardized state implementation that continues to focus on the foundational ideas and powerful representations suggested by national goals and expectations, or does *standardize* contradict *foundational ideas* and *powerful representations?* For instance, rather than a "word wall" for all classrooms being mandated, how about "evidence of the powerful representations of your subject" being mandated for the walls of every classroom? Would this description fit other subjects, or do we need different mandates for different subjects? And if we do, does it mean that we have lost our standardization? And who is it that makes these decisions? Are they trained in policy and leadership or are they trained in content or pedagogy? Do these folks need to be trained in both? Do such people exist, and if so, how many of them are there?

I am now dreaming, can we clean the slate and start over? For instance, can we tell teachers that they have the first two months of school to create relationships with their students within the work of talking about and representing the foundational mathematical ideas of their grade level? Then ask them to share the plan with their administrators along with a plan for reporting the progress they are making at regular time intervals, relieving them of the burden of daily lesson plans, formatted just so, and premade tests at mandated times with no regard for students or their learning. There is nothing so devastating to students' academic self-image as giving a test today that they could ace next week, and having them fail it. Or would this approach in its implementation become as rigid and dogmatic as the mandates we have now rather than creating more space to talk about instruction?

All of this to say, I wonder if there is room for *me* in the classroom anymore? I wonder if there is room for *me* in a state department of education? I wonder if there is room in state policies, guided and partially funded by federal mandates, for others *like me*, who can teach students and allow them to be themselves, their best selves, in a mathematics classroom?

—*Ellen Clay*

References

Anderson, J. D. (2001). Introduction to Part 3: 1950–1980, Separate and unequal. In S. Mondale & S. Patting (Eds.), *School: The story of American public education* (pp. 123–130). Boston, MA: Beacon Press.

Anyon, J. (2005). *Radical possibilities: Public policy, urban education, and a new social movement*. New York, NY: Routledge.

Apple, M. (2001). *Educating the "right" way: Market standards, God and inequality*. New York, NY: Routledge Falmer.

Ashman, B. (Producer), & Sackler, M. (Director) (2010). *The lottery* [Motion Picture]. U.S.A: Breaking Glass Pictures.

Ayers, W. (1998). Foreword: Popular education: Teaching for social justice. In W. Ayers, J. A. Hunt, & T. Quinn (Eds.), *Teaching for social justice: A democracy and education reader* (pp. xvii–xxv). New York, NY: Teachers College Press.

Bambara, T. C. (2004). *Geraldine Moore the poet*. New York, NY: Scholastic Press.

Belfield, C. R., & Levin, H. M (2009). *Market reforms in education*. In G. Sykes, B. Schneider, & D. N. Plank (Eds.), *Handbook of education policy research* (pp. 513–527). New York, NY: Routledge.

Bettie, J. (2003). *Women without class: Girls, race and identity*. Berkeley, CA: University of California Press.

Birtel, M., (Producer) & Guggenheim, D. (Director) & (2010). *Waiting for Superman* [Motion Picture]. Hollywood, CA: Paramount Vantage.

Bruner, J. (1960). *The process of education*. Cambridge, MA: Harvard University Press.

Bryk, A., Camburn, E., & Louis, K. S. (1999). Professional community in Chicago elementary schools: Facilitating factors and organizational consequences. *Educational Administration Quarterly, 35*(5), 751–781.

Bussis, A, Cittenden, E. & Amarel, M. (1976). *Beyond the surface curriculum: An interview study of teachers' understandings*. Boulder, CO: Westview Press.

Carter, P. (2005). *Keepin' it real: School success beyond Black and White*. New York, NY: Oxford University Press.

Center for Research on Education Outcomes (CREDO). (2013). National charter school study. Stanford, CA: Stanford University, CREDO.

Chikkatur, A. P., & Jones-Walker, C. (2013). The influence of researcher identity on ethnographies in multiracial schools. *International Journal of Qualitative Studies in Education, 26*(7), 829–847.

Clotfelter, C. T. (2011). *After "Brown": The rise and retreat of school desegregation*. Princeton, NJ: Princeton University Press.

Cochran-Smith, M. (2004). *Walking the road: Race, diversity and social justice in teacher education.* New York, NY: Teachers College Press.

Cochran-Smith, M., & Lytle, S. L. (2009). *Inquiry as a stance: Practitioner research in the next generation.* New York, NY: Teachers College Press.

Crenshaw, K., Gotanda, N., Peller, G., & Thomas, K. (Eds.). (1995). *Critical race theory: The key writings that formed the movement.* New York, NY: New Press.

Cuban, L. (1986). *Teachers and machines: The classroom use of technology since 1920.* New York, NY: Teachers College Press.

Dance, L. J. (2002). *Tough fronts: The impact of street culture on schooling.* New York, NY: Routledge.

Darling-Hammond, L. (1997). Reforming the school reform agenda: Developing capacity for school transformation. In E. Cinchy (Ed.), *Transforming public education* (pp. 38–55). New York, NY: Teachers College Press.

Darling-Hammond, L., & Berry, B. (2006). Highly qualified teachers for all. *Educational Leadership, 64*(3), 14–20.

Darling- Hammond, L., & McLaughlin, M. W. (1995). Policies that support professional development in an era of reform. *Phi Delta Kappan, 76*(8), 597–604.

Darling-Hammond, L., Newton, S. P., & Wei, R. C. (2013). Developing and assessing beginning teacher effectiveness: The potential of performance assessments. *Educational Assessment, Evaluation and Accountability, 25*(3), 179–204.

Drake, C., Spillane, J., & Hufferd-Ackles, K. (2001). Storied identities: Teacher learning and subject-matter context. *Journal of Curriculum Studies, 33*(1), 1–23.

DuBois, W.E.B. (1899). *The Philadelphia Negro: A social study.* Philadelphia, PA: University of Pennsylvania Press.

DuFour, R. (2004). What is a professional learning community? *Educational Leadership, 61*(8), 6–11.

Duncan, A. (2012, January 6). Escaping the constraints of "No Child Left Behind." *The Washington Post,* Retrieved from www.washingtonpost.com/opinions/escaping-the-constraints-of-no-child-left-behind/2012/01/06/gIQAYmqpfP_story.html

Edmonds, R. (1979). Effective schools for the urban poor. *Educational leadership, 37*(1), 15–24.

Elmore, R. (2002). Getting to scale with good educational practice. *Harvard Educational Review, 66*(1).

Erickson, F. (1982). Qualitative methods in research on teaching. In M. C. Wittrock & American Educational Research Association (Eds.), *Handbook of research on teaching* (3rd ed., pp. xi –1037). New York, NY: Macmillan.

Essed,, P., & Goldberg, D.T. (2002). *Race critical theories: texts and context.* Malden, MA: Blackwell Publishers.

Fang, Z. (1996). A review of research on teacher beliefs and practices. *Educational Research, 38*(1).

Ferguson, A. A. (2001). *Bad boys: Public schools in the making of Black masculinity.* Ann Arbor, MI: University of Michigan Press.

Fiel, J. E. (2013). Decomposing school resegregation: Social closure, racial imbalance, and racial isolation. *American Sociological Review, 78*(5), 828.

Fine, M. (1991). *Framing dropouts: Notes on the politics of an urban high school.* Albany, NY: State University of New York Press.

Foucault, M. (1995). *Discipline and punish: The birth of the prison.* New York, NY: Vintage.

French, D., Miles, K. H., & Nathan, L. (2014). *The path forward: School autonomy and its implications for the future of Boston's public schools.* (Prepared by Educational Resource Strategies and the Center for Collaborative Education for The Boston Foundation and Boston Public Schools.) Boston, MA: The Boston Foundation.

Fuller, B. F., & Elmore, R. (1996). *Who chooses? Who loses? Culture, institutions, and the unequal effects of school choice.* New York, NY: Teachers College Press.

Gee, J. P. (2004). Discourse analysis: What makes it critical? In R. Rogers (Ed.), *An introduction to critical discourse analysis in education* (pp. 19–50). Mahwah, NJ: Erlbaum.

Gee, J. P (2005). *An introduction to discourse analysis: Theory and method* (2nd ed). New York, NY: Routledge.

Gold, E., Lewis, K., Suess, G., Jones-Walker, C., & Rosen, S. (2008). Writing to be heard: A collection of papers by youth researchers doing school organizing (A Research for Action project). In R. Stoecker (Ed.), *COMM-ORG Papers Collection* (Vol.14). Retrieved from comm-org.wisc.edu/papers.htm

Greene, M. (1995). *Releasing the imagination: Essays on education, the arts, and social change,* San Francisco, CA: Jossey-Bass.

Gutierrez, K. D. (1992). A comparison of instructional contexts in writing process classrooms with Latino children. *Education and Urban Society, 24*(2), 244–262.

Hall, S. (1994). Cultural identity and diaspora. In P. Williams & L. Chrisman, (Eds.), *Colonial discourse and post-colonial theory: A reader* (pp. 392–403). New York, NY: Columbia University Press.

Hirschman, A.O. (1970). Exit, voice and loyalty. Cambridge, MA: Harvard University Press.

hooks, b. (2004). *Skin again.* New York, NY: Hyperion for Children.

Ingersoll, R., & Alsalam, N. (1997). Teacher professionalism and teacher commitment: A multilevel analysis (NCES 97-069). *Washington, DC: National Center for Education Statistics.*

Jones-Walker, C. (2008). (Co)constructing identities in urban classrooms. Dissertations available from ProQuest. Paper AAI3309448. Retrieved from repository. upenn.edu/dissertations/AAI3309448/

Karp, S. (2013). The problems with the Common Core. *Rethinking Schools, 28*(2). Retrieved from www.rethinkingschools.org/archive/28_02/28_02_karp.shtml

Ladson-Billings, G. (2009). *The dreamkeepers: Successful teachers of African American children* (2nd ed.). San Francisco, CA: Jossey-Bass.

Lampert, M. (1985). How do teachers manage to teach? Perspectives on problems in practice. *Harvard Educational Review, 55*(2), 178–195.

Levinson, B. A., & Holland, D. (1996). The cultural production of the educated person: An introduction. In B. A. Levinson, D. E. Foley, & D. C. Holland (Eds.), *The cultural production of the educated person: Critical ethnographies of schooling and local practice* (pp. 1–54). Albany, NY: State University of New York Press.

Lewis-Charp, H., Yu, H. C., & Soukamneuth, S. (2006). Civic activist approaches for engaging youth in social justice. In S. Ginwright, P. Noguera, & J. Cammarota (Eds.), *Beyond resistance!: Youth activism and community change* (pp. 21–36). New York, NY: Routledge.

Lipman, P. (2011). *The new political economy of urban education: Neoliberalism, race, and the right to the city.* New York, NY: Routledge.

Little, J. W. (1982). Norms of collegiality and experimentation: Workplace conditions of school success. *American Education Research Journal, 19*(3), 325–340.

Little, J. W. (1993). Teachers' professional development in a climate of educational reform. *Educational Evaluation and Policy Analysis, 15*(2), 129–151.

Massey, D. S., & Denton, N. A. (1993). *American apartheid: Segregation and the making of the underclass.* Harvard University Press.

McAdams, D. P. (1993). *The stories we live by: Personal myths and the making of the self.* New York, NY: Morrow.

McCarthy, S. (2001). Identity construction in elementary readers and writers. *Reading Research Quarterly, 36*(2). 122–151.

McCarthey, S. J., & Moje, E. B. (2002). Identity matters. *Reading Research Quarterly, 37*(2), 228–238.

McMahon, B., & Portelli, J. P. (2004). Engagement for what? Beyond popular discourses of student engagement. *Leadership & Policy in Schools, 3*(1), 59–76.

Mediratta, K., Shah, S., & McAlister, S. (2009). *Community organizing for stronger schools: strategies and successes.* Cambridge, MA: Harvard Education.

Mintrop, H., & Sunderman, G. L. (2009). Predictable failure of federal sanctions-driven accountability for school improvement—and why we may retain it anyway. *Educational Researcher, 38*(5), 353–364.

Mondale, S., & Patton, S. (2001). "Why don't you go to school with us?" In S. Mondale & S. Patting (Eds.), *School: The story of American public education* (pp.131–170). Boston, MA: Beacon Press.

National Commission on Excellence in Education. (1983). A nation at risk: The imperative for educational reform. *The Elementary School Journal,* 113–130.

Nespor, J. (1987). The role of beliefs in the practice of teaching. *Journal of Curriculum Studies, 19*(4), 317–328.

Newman, F. M. (1989). Student engagement and high school reform. *Educational Leadership, 46*(5), 34–36.

Nieto, S. (1996). *Affirming diversity: The sociopolitical context of multicultural education.* New York, NY: Longman.

Noguera, P. A. (2003). *City schools and the American dream: Fulfilling the promise of public education.* New York, NY: Teachers College Press.

Oakes, J., Franke, M. L., Quartz, K. H., & Rogers, J. (2002). Research for high-quality urban teaching: Defining it, developing it, assessing it. *Journal of Teacher Education, 53*(3), 228–234.

Oakes, J., Rogers, J., with Lipton, M. (2006). *Learning power: Organizing for education and justice.* New York, NY: Teachers College Press.

Orfield, G. (2009). Foreword. In H. Mintrop & G. L. Sunderman, *Why high stakes accountability sounds good but doesn't work—and why we keep on doing it anyway.* Los Angeles, CA: The Civil Rights Project/Proyecto Derechos Civiles at UCLA.

Orfield, G., Siegel-Hawley, G., & Kucsera, J. (2014, March). *Sorting out deepening confusion on segregation trends.* Los Angeles, CA: The Civil Rights Project/Proyecto Derechos Civiles at UCLA.

Parise, L. M., & Spillane, J. P. (2010). Teacher learning and instructional change: How formal and on-the-job learning opportunities predict change in elementary school teachers' practice. *The Elementary School Journal*, *110*(3), 323–346.

Payne, C. M. (2008). *So much reform, so little change: The persistence of failure in urban schools*. Cambridge, MA: Harvard Education Press.

Pearson, L. C., & Moomaw, W. (2005). The relationship between teacher autonomy and stress, work satisfaction, empowerment, and professionalism. *Educational Research Quarterly*, *29*(1), 38–54.

Perkinson, H. (1968). *The imperfect panacea*. New York, NY: Random House.

Perry, T., Moses, R. P., Cortes Jr, E., Delpit, L., & Wynne, J. T. (2010). *Quality education as a constitutional right: Creating a grassroots movement to transform public schools*. Boston, MA: Beacon Press.

Perry, T., Steele, C., & Hilliard, A., III. (2003) *Young, gifted and Black: Promoting high achievement among African American students*. Boston, MA: Beacon Press.

Polikoff, M. S., McEachin, A. J., Wrabel, S. L., & Duque, M. (2014). The waive of the future? School accountability in the waiver era. *Educational Researcher*, *43*(1), 45–54.

Pollock, M. (2001). How the question we ask most about race in education is the very question we most suppress. *Educational Researcher, 30*(9), 2–11.

Pollock, M. (2005). *Colormute: Race talk dilemmas in an American school*. Princeton, NJ: Princeton University Press.

Query, J. L., Kreps, G. L, Arneson, P., & Caso, N. S. (2001). Toward helping organizations manage interaction: The theoretical and pragmatic merits of the critical incident technique. In S. L. Herndon & G. L. Kreps (Eds.), *Qualitative research: Applications in organizational life* (2nd ed., pp. 91–119). Creskill, NJ: Hampton Press.

Ravitch, D. (2011). *The death and life of the great American school system: How testing and choice are undermining education* (rev. and exp. ed.). New York, NY: Basic Books.

Reardon, S. F., Grewal, E. T., Kalogrides, D., & Greenberg, E. (2012). Brown fades: The end of court-ordered school desegregation and the resegregation of American public schools. *Journal of Policy Analysis and Management, 31*(4), 876–904.

Reich, R. B. (2012). *Beyond outrage: What has gone wrong with our economy and our democracy, and how to fix it*. New York, NY: Vintage Books.

Reich, R. B. (2014, June 13). The three biggest right-wing lies about poverty [Blog post]. Retrieved from robertreich.org/post/88708262000

Reville, P., with Coggins, C. (Eds.). (2007). *A decade of urban school reform: persistence and progress in Boston public schools*. Cambridge, MA: Harvard Education Press.

Richardson, V. (1996). The role of attitudes and beliefs in learning to teach. *Handbook of Research on Teacher Education, 2*, 102–119.

Schultz, K. (2003). *Listening: A framework for teaching across differences*. New York, NY: Teachers College Press.

Schultz, K., Jones-Walker, C. E., & Chikkatur, A. (2008). Listening to students, negotiating beliefs: Preparing teachers for urban classrooms. *Curriculum Inquiry, 38*(2), 155–187.

Sizer, T. R. (1984). *Horace's compromise: The dilemma of the American high school*. New York, NY: Houghton Mifflin.

Spencer, M. B., & Markstrom-Adams, C. (1990). Identity process among racial and ethnic minority children in America. *Child Development, 61*(2), 290–310.

Suess, G. E., & Lewis, K. S. (2007). The time is now: Youth organizing to transform Philadelphia schools. *Children Youth and Environments, 17*(2), 364–379.

Swanson, D. P., Spencer, M. B., Dell'Angelo, T., Harpalani, V., & Spencer, T. R. (2002). Identity processes and the positive youth development of African Americans: An explanatory framework. *New directions for youth development, 95,* 73–100.

Tamir, E. (2009). Choosing to teach in urban schools among graduates of elite colleges. *Urban Education, 44*(5), 522–544.

Tamir, E. (2013). *CETE's urban teacher leadership initiative, final evaluation report.* Waltham, MA: Brandeis University.

Varenne, H., & McDermott, R. (1999). *Successful failure: The school America builds.* Boulder, CO: Westview Press.

Welner, K. G., & Carter, P. L. (2013). Achievement gaps arise from opportunity gaps. In P. L. Carter & K. G. Welner (Eds.), *Closing the opportunity gap: What America must do to give every child an even chance* (pp. 1–10). New York, NY: Oxford University Press.

Westheimer, J., & Kahne, J. (1998). Education for action: Preparing youth for participatory democracy. In W. Ayers, J. Hunt, & T. Quinn (Eds.), *Teaching for social justice: A democracy and education reader* (pp. 1–20). New York, NY: Teachers College Press.

Wilson, B. L., & Corbett, H. D. (2001). *Listening to urban kids: School reform and the teachers they want.* Albany, NY: State University of New York Press.

Wortham, S.E.F. (2006). *Learning identity: The joint emergence of social identification and academic learning.* Cambridge, UK: Cambridge University Press.

Index

About the Author

Cheryl Jones-Walker is an associate professor of educational studies on leave from Swarthmore College. She holds a PhD in Foundations and Practices of Education from the University of Pennsylvania. Currently she is a visiting associate professor in the teacher education department at the University of San Francisco. She has worked as a teacher, as a facilitator for school-based reforms efforts, and as an organizer for various educational campaigns. Her research is focused on the examination of identities on macro- and microlevels in order to design the best supports for learners and to address larger sociohistorical issues that undermine opportunities for individuals who have been marginalized.